Muse on Madison Avenue

Studien zur klassischen Philologie

Herausgegeben von Prof. Dr. Michael von Albrecht

Band 127

Peter Lang

Frankfurt am Main · Berlin · Bern · Bruxelles · New York · Oxford · Wien

Karelisa V. Hartigan

Muse on Madison Avenue

Classical Mythology in Contemporary Advertising

Peter Lang
Europäischer Verlag der Wissenschaften

Die Deutsche Bibliothek - CIP-Einheitsaufnahme

Hartigan, Karelisa V.:

Muse on Madison Avenue : classical mythology in contemporary advertising / Karelisa V. Hartigan. - Frankfurt am Main ; Berlin ; Bern ; Bruxelles ; New York ; Oxford ; Wien : Lang, 2002
(Studien zur klassischen Philologie ; Bd. 127)
ISBN 3-631-37652-9

ISSN 0172-1798
ISBN 3-631-37652-9
US-ISBN 0-8204-5367-6

www.peterlang.de

PREFACE

Leafing through a popular magazine some years ago, I stopped suddenly at an advertisement for Paloma Picasso's new fragrance for men, *Minotaure*. As a teacher of classical mythology I recognized the name and the intent of the illustration, a heroic figure looking through a heavy stone doorway. And I also knew that Picasso had created several pictures titled "Minotaur." But, I wondered, for whom was this cologne created, to whom was this advertisement directed? Was the ancient Greek legend of theMinotaur so widely known that name and ad would draw men to the sales counter? And, even if the name was familiar, what was the aroma of a scent named for a mythical beast, half man, half bull, the result of a crazed passion of a Cretan queen?

My reading of popular magazines became different: now I looked carefully at the advertisements, I no longer passed over them on my way to the articles. And it seemed that there were many references to the world of ancient Greek and Roman myth in the creations coming from Madison Avenue. I began to include these advertisements in my lectures to the mythology classes, then I enlisted the help of my students in finding such ads, as they read magazines that would never cross my path. A trend appeared.

Then, as I often do, I presented a paper on my discovery at a professional meeting and the topic was enthusiastically received. Colleagues around the nation began to send me further examples, my files and slide trays burgeoned with advertisements inspired by ancient myth. Dennis Hall, editor of *Studies in Popular Culture,* shepherded an early article into print. My husband, himself author of some two dozen books, was sure there was material for a book. And so this study was born.

In the writing of *Muse on Madison Avenue*, I owe appreciation to many people. First I must include those students and colleagues who joined in my project. But there are always those who deserve my special acknowledgment. Several student assistants helped me collect material: Sarah Crawford, Carol Davis, Julie Williams and, in particular, Wesley Harvin, were exceptionally helpful. The reference staff at the library patiently answered my requests for company addresses. James Twitchell, Professor of English who teaches courses in advertising here at the University of Florida, and whose fine book, *Adcult USA,* is often quoted in these pages, advised me as I, a classicist, entered into the realm of popular culture. My greatest debt of assistance is owed to the Classics secretary Kimberly Mansfield, who masterfully and cheerfully put the manuscript into proper final format. No words can adequately express my gratitude to her. Most of all, however, I acknowledge the encouragement and patience of my husband as I worked on this book, filling our computer room with glossy advertisements; I also appreciate the fact that he never mocked my progress as he completed six books while I finished just this one. So, once again, my book is dedicated to him.

For Kevin

CONTENTS

MUSE ON MADISON AVENUE
I
CLASSICAL MYTHOLOGY IN CONTEMPORARY ADVERTISING.

INTRODUCTION

While the usual quest is for truth in advertising, my pursuit is for myth in advertising. In a culture which promotes, indeed, adulates, the new, and from which traditional classical learning is ever more absent, within the last several years an abundance of print media advertisements based on the ancient legends of Greece and Rome has appeared. It has been said that advertising "is closely linked to the ideology of a culture, reflecting its values through signs and symbols."[1] Thus the question arises: Why do product promoters turn to classical myths for marketing inspiration? Since the creator of a new ad is trying to reach as many people as possible, what collective awareness is addressed, or what common cultural denomination is assumed? It seems that the mythic legacy of ancient Greece and Rome is still considered to be a part of American (and international) tradition and through advertising it has infiltrated the realm of popular culture.

In antiquity the myths served as paradigms of behavior or, more often, of behavior to be avoided. Through the lens of myth, the taboo could be viewed and its consequences illustrated. The extravagant details added spice to the tales, making them enjoyable and hence memorable. In a culture where genealogy determined social position, divine ancestry enhanced a family's status. That Zeus was said to have visited Leda and engendered Helen and Polydeuces while in the form of a swan made the story titillating, ensuring that it would be remembered. Bizarre details of the myths maintained their popularity after their instructional function had faded; although belief in the ancient gods passed away, the appeal of the ancient tales remained. We know readers in the Middle Ages enjoyed Ovid's texts, but with the tales retold and revised to be suitable for a Christian audience. It is common knowledge that with the dawn of the Renaissance artists turned to classical myth as a cover to paint the human form unclothed: the mythic veil covered the contemporary nude.

---

[1] Rita C. Hubbard, "Shock Advertising: The BENETTON Case," *SPC* 16 (1993): 39.

In the world of modern advertising, the mythmaking operators of Madison Avenue can use a classical name to enhance the suggestive names of products, to underscore an idea the manufacturer wants to imply. Thus a perfume explicitly named, for example, *Desire* or *Tabu*, can be advertised with an image of Aphrodite, the love goddess, to show its erotic power, or with figures illustrating the Pygmalion myth to suggest the perfume provokes a secret romance between artist and creation. Clothing shown on models in the ecstatic dance of a Maenad, a follower of Dionysus, suggests the buyer may also be swayed by the power of that god of nature and emotion. An advertisement that portrays the model as earnest and respectful implies that the one who wears this brand will be so also.

Other advertisements use the ancient legends to give the product status.[2] *Classic* still describes any lasting ideal, any object with true quality, and few can deny that classic most commonly refers in the western world to ideals derived from ancient Greece and Rome. A revered object is not placed upon a tree stump, totem pole, or a ladder: instead its pedestal is a Doric or Ionic column. In recent advertisements, REMY MARTIN Cognac stands atop a Doric capital, an ACURA parks between two classic columns, while the image of the Medici Venus appears with a MAZDA. As Jackson Lears pointed out, the advertisers, by promoting their products with a seemingly traditional aura, "scrambled past and present, stripped material goods of their actual historical associations, and allowed them to enter a sphere where the object itself was less important than the desires that could be projected onto it."[3]

The assumption of a common cultural core also permits the advertiser to appeal to an equally common desire to be thought cultured; snob appeal underlies many advertising campaigns. Ads reproduce classic symbols and statues as echoes,

---

[2] Although Paul Marciano said of his GUESS TV commercials "We don't think that deeply when we create a film" (i.e., a commercial, a word Marciano eschews, "I don't like to call it a commercial. It's a small film"), I think we can give greater credit to the creative admaker. It is through the association with the classic that a new product gains (instant) status. Furthermore, GUESS print advertisements, in the 1990s at least (as we shall see in chapter IV) are some of the most thought-provoking, so I think we can give Marciano's statement less credibility. Paul Marciano, quoted (without reference) by Leslie Savan in *The Sponsored Life* (Philadelphia: Temple University Press, 1994): 30.

[3] Jackson Lears, *Fables of Abundance. A Cultural History of Advertising in America.* (New York: Basic Books 1994): 385.

if not replicas, of art objects collected in museums or in the homes of the rich and famous. The glossy magazine advertisements provide framed images that are stand ins for high art. As one scholar of popular culture puts it, the magazines "have become petite galleries of 'high art,' postmodern transformations . . . of constantly shifting artistic memories."[4] A final permutation of the concept of ad as art has recently emerged. In 1994 a company taking the name "beyond the wall" came into being, a poster company dedicated to "redefining poster art" by seeing "ads as art." The New Hampshire based business, catering especially to college students, offers the best or most provocative advertisements as posters to adorn dorm room walls. Ads thus replace traditional prints as college decorations, students of the 1990s recognize DKNY's Jeans of New York or Davidoff's *Cool Water* more easily than Van Gogh's *Sunflowers* or Monet's Sunrise series.

Advertisements vying for our attention have become the basis of a new cultural literacy for our society. According to Ronald Berman,Americans worry about the relationship of present to future, where we have been, what we will become. "These great themes of the imagination, once in the province of literature, have now become part of advertising. The fact is that advertising does much more than persuade us to consume goods and services: It tells us who we are."[5] The colorful pages of images also, in a way, serve to create a new mythology: purchasing the various touted products will enable the buyer to achieve what Madison Avenue has determined is everyone's goal: a life filled with sex, beauty, and membership in a culturally exclusive club; the product itself defines the type of club. "Commercials and other forms of product advertising," writes Berman, "are not so much about inducements to buy goods as they are statements about why goods are produced, whom they benefit, and how they fit into our lives."[6]

The advertisements discussed here use ancient myth to create this modern myth: a sort of ring-composition, itself certainly a classic trope. The cultural club to which the mythic ads offer the key is based on tradition and the status associated with knowledge of that tradition, the mythology of Greece and Rome.

Recently a new type of promotional approach has appeared: the ad as

[4] Dennis Hall, "Advertising as High Art," *The Mid-Atlantic Almanack* 4 (1995): 54-60.

[5] Ronald Berman, *Advertising and Social Change.* (Beverly Hills: Sage Publications, 1981): 12.

[6] Berman, *Advertising*: 102.

narrative. NIKE took this style to a new level: five, six, even ten pages of text described the heights able to be achieved by wearers of the NIKE sneaker. The company addressed both men and women, offering a different narrative for men and women, a difference determined by the magazine's intended readership. In the 1994 campaigns, men were advised to live well—and have heroes. The ads directed at women began, "You are not a goddess." This very modern shoe promotion started from an ancient assumption, while the shadow image behind the text suggested the female NIKE wearer really does resemble an ancient deity. As the text unfolded, we learned that the woman walking in a NIKE could accomplish feats that would render her nearly divine: while the opening line avoided classical hubris, the text elevated the woman to full potential. How very Greek: to be god-like, but not to be assumed a god. And the whole advertisement was a mini-story, about the length of a passage from Ovid's *Metamorphosis*. NIKE eschewed pictures for text while busy developing the NIKE myth. NIKE's name and symbol are Greek: the wing represents that of the Winged Goddess of Victory, *Nike*. The company's logo shows its desire to be victorious and swift in its race to victory. Thus it is appropriate that NIKE seek to create a modern mythology to underline its own meaning.

Sometimes a company chooses to use advertisements to make a social statement. The best known, if not to say notorious, is the social awareness campaign launched by BENETTON in 1984. Begun in an effort to promote multi-culturalism and break down racial prejudices, the company published a series of ever more shocking photos, on which the only text is "United Colors of BENETTON." The images were chosen for a carefully targeted audience, intended to arouse social consciousness by the explicit pictures.[7]

Although Benetton may have gone to the limit, other companies have followed suit in trying to catch the public eye by suggestive images and/or statements. Thus in its 1993-94 advertisements for its JOOP! jeans, the Jonbil company ran a series of illustrations that have nothing to do with jeans; indeed, no pair appears in the advertisement at all. Instead, we were offered a picture of Eros/Cupid, lying supine before us, pierced in the back with one of his own arrows.[8] The text read: "WE HAVE DEGREES FOR MURDER BUT NOT FOR

---

[7] Hubbard, *SPC* 16: 39-51. By 1993-1994, Benetton had gone so far in its pictures that customers began to rebel against the company because of its advertisements. Even those who bought an item made by Benetton refused to take it out in a store shopping bag. Information cited from Anne Sengès, "United Colors: La Fin d'un Mythe," *Journal Français d'Amérique* (9/ 16-29): 5.

[8] The Eros wounded advertisements were published in many magazines targeted for an

LOVE. JUST A THOUGHT!" This "Just A Thought" series was intended to make its audience have exactly that; perhaps the thought would carry over to the purchase of a pair of JOOP! jeans.[9]

In his excellent study of advertising in American culture, *Adcult USA*, James Twitchell argues several times for a similarity between religion and advertising. Having quoted Leo Burnett's statement on the need for magic in advertising's words, Twitchell suggests that we seek redemption through purchase as earlier peoples had sought it through faith: we expect the figures of advertising to have the powers of the ancient gods:

> The ability to coax beneficent spirits from their habitations was very much a part of classical beliefs.These spirits, be they gods, dryads, nymphs, or mythic personages with names like Zeus, Hera, Jupiter, and Ajax, became the saints, cherubs, and seraphim of the Christian heavens. The Jolly Green Giant, the Michelin Man, the Man from Glad, Mother Nature, Aunt Jemima...and all their otherworldly kin are descendants of the earlier gods. What separates them is that they now reside in manufactured products and that, although earlier gods were invoked by fasting, prayer, rituals, and penance, the promise of purchase calls forth their modern ilk.[10]

Ronald Berman expressed similar ideas. The overt statements of ads are accompanied by silent messages that reflect basic truths of human life: protective motherhood, inevitability of both change and death, people are all the same; commercials about soap are also "about ethnic equality, reverence for the past, and the values of our civil religion."[11]

Advertising is the common cultural understanding of contemporary America. No one would dispute the ways in which products ads have become part of modern American speech and instantly recognizable visual images. Twitchell points out that his students can easily complete advertising tunes or jingles but not the more

---

upscale audience; cf. Elle (November, 1993). For image, see Illustration 3.29.

[9] A further example of this "Just a Thought" series appears in Chapter IV.

[10] James Twitchell, *Adcult USA. The Triumph of Advertising in American Culture*. (New York: Columbia University Press 1996): 30.

[11] Berman, *Advertising*: 113.

famous lines of English poetry.[12] Nevertheless, I argue here that underlying many contemporary advertisements are the icons of the earliest days of western culture. When E.D. Hirsch raised both desires and hackles by offering a list of "What Every American Needs to Know" (implying "ought to know") so that we, sharing what Hirsch calls "cultural literacy" can engage in "effective communication," included in what we (ought to) know were the figures and legends collected in Greek and Roman mythology.[13] While the backlash and rebellion against this "list" was strong, widely publicized, and led to the creating of still other lists, those who must deal most urgently and most immediately with the American shopper have clearly assumed that the ancient myths are part of modern culture. To understand the messages communicated by the advertisements for products from bras to brandy, from cars to condoms, from plates to perfumes, one must know the legends coming to twentieth century America from classical Greece and Rome.

Why the Classical myths appeal.

In her book titled *Hidden Myth*, Varda Langholz-Leymore argues that "advertising plays the same role in modern societies that myth performs in other societies." Rather than being a source for social change, Leymore asserts, advertising supports the social order by reducing anxieties and providing simple solutions for eternal human dilemmas.[14] If this and other studies which apply the methodology and assumptions of anthropology and psychology to the topic are correct, it should be no surprise to discover that ancient myth and modern advertising are linked; classical myth is an appropriate arena for those wishing to promote the good life in today's world. From all the evidence presented in recent magazines, the Muse is alive and well on Madison Avenue. Can we find any reasons this is so?

Thomas Levitt has argued that advertising, like art, enhances life by offering an enhanced world: reality is dull, but art and advertising alike suggest something higher.[15] Dennis Hall noted that the glossy pictures in modern advertising might be

---

[12] Twitchell, *Adcult*: 4.

[13] E.D. Hirsch, Jr. *Cultural Literacy: What Every American Needs to Know.* (New York: Houghton Mifflin, 1987).

[14] Varda Langholz-Leymore, *Hidden Myth: Structure and Symbolism in Advertising*, (London: Heinemann Educational Books, 1975): ix-x.

[15] Theodore Levitt, "The Morality (?) of Advertising," *Harvard Business Review* (July-

considered stand-ins for high art, framed on the page, not on the wall, but frequently as visually pleasing.[16] Certainly when the ad makers turn to classical myth, they have an entre into the art world because the classical subject has already been recognized and acclaimed as art. Levitt further argues that ad men, like poets and playwrights, deal in symbolic communication, their communication "is a creative conceptualization that implies a vicarious experience through symbolic substitutes." The intent of advertising, like that of art, is to "embellish, enhance, and illuminate."[17]

Thomas Hine points out that images become icons for a variety of reasons, some better than others.[18] Familiarity does breed reuse, and thus quotations, both aural and visual, can become clichés. But reuse is successful because of the immediate recognition: images serve as a kind of short hand for those who need to communicate quickly; thus has advertising pounced upon so many images of modern culture, those based on actual events and artifacts as well as those based on myth. But there is, I think, something further than easy access via instant recognition. The images that reappear also communicate our cultural values and self-awareness. The symbols by which a culture chooses to express itself reflect its deepest values.

Jennifer Wicke asserts that as every cultural artifact is "produced by individual makers, by institutional settings, by collective aspirations and values. . . by its adoption and use by a public, and by its place in an overall political economy," so is an advertisement.[19] She continues:

> Advertising's cultural tasks are many. In the absence of a personalized market, it must compensate for older forms, like the

---

August, 1972), rep. *Advertising's Role in Society,* ed. J. S. Wright and J. E. Mertes (St. Paul, MN: West Publishing, 1974): 278-289. Levitt argues that advertising is like poetry: its purpose "is to influence an audience; to affect its perceptions and sensibilities."

[16] Hall, "Advertising as High Art," *MAA* 4 (1995): 54-60.

[17] Levitt, "Morality(?)": 280-281.

[18] Thomas Hine, "Notable Quotables: Why Images Become Icons," *New York Times* (February 18, 1996): 1/37.

[19] Jennifer Wicke, *Advertising Fictions. Literature, Advertisement, & Social Reading.* (New York: Columbia, 1988): 16. Her study is of literature as advertising, advertising as literature and the importance of both in any society.

> buying fairs with their carnivalesque elements of exchange. Vanished human relations of exchange and barter are compensated for within advertisement... Where channels of public speech have broken down—the church pulpit, the town meeting—advertisements' illusory surface of collective discourse finds a place. Finally, within advertisements themselves the culture finds a location for staging the contradiction inherent in the myths of general desire.[20]

As we shall see here, to stage the myths of our desires effectively, the creator of contemporary advertisements turns frequently to the most ancient legends of western culture, those told first by the Greeks and Romans.

Leo Burnett, head of one of the most successful advertising agencies ever, established for his employees a "check list" to guide them in creating successful ads. Under his first rubric he wrote: "Don't tell people how good you make goods; tell them how good your goods make them."[21] That is exactly what the advertisements based upon the classical legends do. The association of the potential buyer with the implications of the product must rest upon recognized images. As Andrew Wernick has pointed out, products valorized by symbols can only work if the symbolism employed is intelligible. Symbolic ads "must build up significance from elements of an understood cultural code," and the values by which the product is endorsed must rest upon values which appeal to the society for which the product is designed.[22] Those who create advertisements assume we have the cultural literacy that E.D. Hirsch, Jr. described as necessary, that we have accumulated "shared symbols and the shared information that the symbols represent," that when we understand what someone is saying, we understand more than the surface

---

[20] Wicke: 16-17. Note her use of "carnivalesque." One does not have to read very far in advertising texts or histories to discover the idea of carnival culture plays a major role.

[21] This rubric in its entirety was: Emotionalize: Offer the reader something in terms of one of the two basic laws of human nature: (A) Self-Preservation, (B) Self-Enhancement. Quoted from Leo Burnett, "A Check-list for a Successful Advertisement," excerpted from Leo Burnett, *Communications of an Advertising Man* (Chicago: Leo Burnett Co. 1961): 243-245, rep. in John S. Wright and John E. Mertes, *Advertising's Role in Society*, (St. Paul: West Publishing 1974): 226.

[22] Andrew Wernick, *Promotional Culture. Advertising, ideology and symbolic expression.* (London: Sage Publications, 1991): 37-38.

meaning of the words; we understand the context as well.[23]

Some companies have created recognized images, in the parlance of advertising called VI/Ps, Visual Image/Personalities, to make their products readily identifiable. Others companies have opted to promote their product by turning to already existing visual images, images that have always been part of our human psyche. It is well-known that the classical myths underlie both western art and western psychological understanding. The ad makers of Madison Avenue have drawn the inspiration for their print media advertisements from the familiar yet deep recesses of the human soul. In the following chapters I illustrate how the creators of contemporary advertisements have brought the classical Muse to Madison Avenue.

[23] Hirsch, *Cultural Literacy*: xvii & 3.

II
HISTORICAL BACKGROUND
AN OVERVIEW OF MYTHS IN ADS FROM THE 1950s TO THE 1990s

Advertising, as reflective of its times, has always used images intended to fulfill the expectations of its buyers. In earlier days, it did not seek to lure customers with shocking illustrations, nor present an ambiguous image suggesting something other than a straightforward invitation to use the product. Thus during the 1950s and into 1960s, full page ads were content to present an outfit, a bottle of perfume, a nightdress, a hairstyle. The product was the image. To enhance that image, however, companies' ad men sought to promote the idea that their goods were worthy of respect as classics. Name as well as picture were chosen to recall works of art venerated as part of western civilized tradition. Thus the advertisement was designed to show a product both as an enhancement of life now and reflective of established ideas of the classic.

Art as attractive visuals is not, of course, the initial or final aim of advertising. Ads are created to sell products. According to a *Fortune* magazine article (November, 1947), the primary cultural function of advertising is "the creation of new and daring, but fulfillable, consumer demands; demands that would not occur if advertising did not deliberately incite them."[1] And, as we shall see here, the admakers turn to classical art for illustrations to arouse this desire for the new. To this end another aspect of ancient culture underlies the very premise and purpose of advertising: rhetoric. Rhetoric is persuasive speaking, and this, persuasion, is the real intent of advertising. Whether it be hidden, as Vance Packard declared when he alarmed the American public in his 1957 book, *The Hidden Persuaders*, or overt, as more recent scholars of advertising argue, no one would displace persuasion from its primary position in the world created by Madison Avenue. The writers of Greece, in particular, recognized that *Peitho*, persuasion, was a dangerous goddess. In his *Agamemnon*, Aeschylus defines her as "the daughter of designing Ruin" (385-86) and it takes the length of the *Oresteia* trilogy to work out an acceptable practice of persuasion. But *Peitho's* power was also celebrated by Athenian authors. Isocrates (15.254) writes that it is "by the power of persuasive speech" that man is distinguished from animals and, by implication, that speakers of Attic Greek are distinguished from barbarians. This book points out

[1] "J. Walter Thompson Company," *Fortune* (November, 1947: 210), cited by Thomas Frank, *The Conquest of Cool* (Chicago: University of Chicago 1997): 49.

how ancient art has been used for product promotion, but the fact remains and must be remembered that ancient art is used by the modern advertiser in the service of the equally ancient art of rhetoric, the art of persuasion.

In this chapter I turn back the pages of advertising and consider earlier examples of classical myth in mid-20th century print media. The greatest number of examples come from perfume ads, although women's clothing and lingerie also supply a goodly number. The explicit nature of more recent advertising has not always been in style. In the advertisements appearing in *Vogue* or *Glamour*, for instance, in the 1950s and early 1960s, clothing was shown on models standing alone, or as worn by well-known figures of society. The models were beautiful but it was the clothes which received the attention. Perfume was promoted with pictures of flowers or lace curtains; usually the vial stood alone, a shape and name to be quickly recognized as it stood on a store's display counter.

In due time those who created the product promotions wanted more timeless and universal themes for their illustrations. Familiar figures of classical art, the images of ancient deities, as well as the acclaimed structures erected for these divinities, the masterpieces of classical architecture, offered them inspiration. They could give their product immediate status by adorning its advertisement with an example commonly recognized as "the classic." Whether the object promoted is a brandy, a car, a cigarette, a nightgown, a swimsuit, or a plumbing fixture, it can be enhanced when a Greek or Roman statue or column is part of the illustration. Thus did classical myth enter into print-media advertisements.

Women's Attire

Grecian lines dominated the styles of the 1950s and 1960s. Models wearing gowns for dinner and gowns for the bedroom, gowns frequently named for the goddess of love, posed in front of columns and in the company of classic statues. Page after page of the fashion magazines were emblazoned with images from the ancient world, occasionally from Rome but more frequently from Greece. Although the West's intellectual debt to classical Greece had long been recognized, in these years the small country in the Aegean had just been discovered as a tourist destination. Greece was a romantic place, still exotic, a place of beauty. History and locale could enhance a product: the history was familiar, the terrain new and beautiful. The rich and famous went to Greece (in reality archaeologists did too, but those who worked in Greece did not wear designer clothes). The woman who purchased a product advertised in Grecian terms could partake of the jetset life, even if her actual involvement might be no more than wearing a Venus gown to bed.

In the following pages I offer a small but representative sample of the many advertisements of the 1950s and 1960s that turned to Greece and the idea of the Classic it embodied for their inspiration. Then I review the influence of specific deities upon advertising copy. Finally, to show how the theme has been continuous, the advertising history of three perfumes is also outlined here.

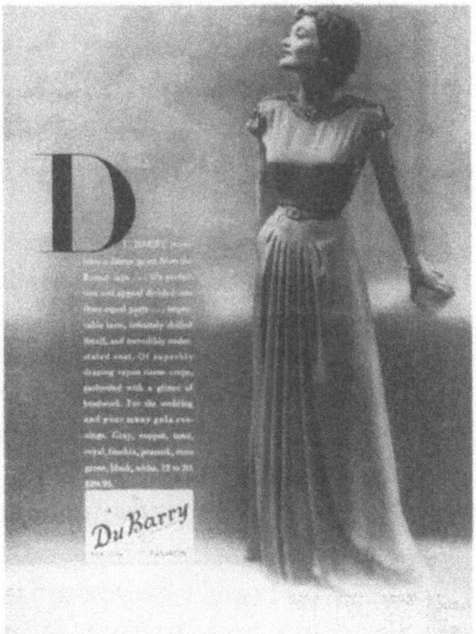

2.1 Du Barry: Gown

In the late summer of 1950, Du Barry "translate[d] a dinner gown from the Roman toga...."[2] The superbly draped rayon tissue crepe, available in 9 colors (including gray, copper, royal, fuschia, black and white) was adorned across neck and shoulders with a "glitter of beadwork." The gown, which was very attractive and sold for the "incredibly understated cost" of $29.95, was not, however, immediately derived from the Roman toga, although perhaps from the Roman stola. The simplicity of the bodice was striking and in nice contrast to the full·skirt which flowed in graceful folds from a dropped waist. Whether or not the gown was directly based on Roman dress, its simple elegance surely proclaimed it worthy of the adjective classic. What is of interest, of course, is that the designer of this Du Barry dress had fallen under the spell of the Roman world which so influenced fashion design at the time.

In 1955 Greta Plattry turned to classic architecture to promote its new fashions. In a multi-page advertisement the company set its new "Aegean Pearls" line amid ruins and scenes from Greece.[3] Plattry used various fabrics (which made the advertisements dual purpose) for designs supposedly inspired by the Greek islands. Sometimes the models were set before a ruin of a Greek temple superimposed upon a rocky landscape, at other times the women were backed by several temple pictures. Each outfit claimed an aspect of the landscape for its

[2] It was advertised in magazines, including *Vogue*, in August, 1950.

[3] The advertisement appeared in *Vogue* (January 15, 1955).

design. "Dodecanese" put its rich golden embroidery on dresses in "island colors," a Maxwell® silk was imprinted with windmills from the island of Mykonos, a Springmaid® combed lawn cotton was gathered into pleats inspired by classic columns (site not identified). Several ruined temples backed the only dresses that truly looked Greek in inspiration, a Dazzle® cotton embroidered with the Greek key in gold. Grecian jugs formed the print design on a sundress and bathing suit in Everglaze® cotton created by Ameritex while the final Aegean Pearl, also created by Ameritex and also in Everglaze® cotton, was a sundress and fustanella adorned with "stripes of hibiscus from the Island of Rhodes"; the models stood on a beach backed by three sets of column pictures.

A single full-page ad, later in the same January 1955 issue, promoted Greta Plattry's Aegean shirts, which did have a rather classical line created by a series of pleats, but the tapered striped slacks, which the text stated were "taken from the Greek," showed no obvious Greek influence. The models were on horseback before the Temple of Concordia at Agrigento in Sicily. In these advertisements full use was made of the classic ideal; anything Greek-islands, windmills, amphoras or flowers--demanded the photographer add the ruins for which Greece is famous. The setting gave the dresses an enhanced cachet: while design and material pattern could have stood alone, the temple columns added class and distinction to the dresses. The woman who bought these outfits would be dressed in enduring style. This belief in the Grecian temple to give lasting value to an outfit (or almost any product) would continue throughout the next fifty years, the old would remain forever current as a metaphor for quality, an instant telegraphing of what modern America considers valuable.

One fashion designer devoted her life to creating the Grecian style for the modern world. For more than 50 years Madame Alix Grès draped her materials to look like an ancient Grecian gown. Her pleating looked "like water flowing from an urn," wrote Dana Thomas in describing her work. Her impact on the fashion world never faltered, her Grecian gowns were for eternity, not for the moment. Although Madame Grès died broken and penniless in 1993 in Provence, the other greats of the fashion world recognized her expertise and the value of her creative work.[4]

In the 1970s, when the female body was to be enhanced by various supporting and confining undergarments, many companies created bras, girdles and

[4] Information from Dana Thomas, "Amazing Grès," *New York Times Magazine* (13 September, 1998): 87. While other designers looked to Greece for occasional inspiration, Madame Grès looked nowhere else.

corsets to restrain any unwanted flesh. In the fall of 1970, Vanity Fair introduced a one-piece bodysuit and advertised it as "Sylph control."[5] The single garment a "line of beauty: sleeker than your own shape, smoother than your own skin" was said to be so light the wearer would hardly know it was there. It is the lightness of the material that creates the mythic reference, for the sylph was an elemental soulless being said to inhabit the air. Although the sylph first appears in late Latin legend, the word comes to describe a graceful young girl, and thus the advertisement is effective on two levels. The model's floating pose suggests she is part of a realm beyond that of the everyday world, while the reality of the garment implies that such grace is available to a an ordinary mortal.

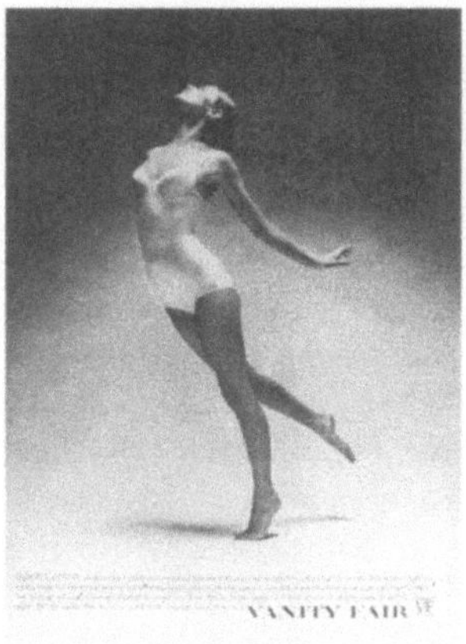

2.2 Vanity Fair: Bodysuit

As one might expect, the bathing suit was a natural to be advertised with a classical sculpture to indicate the suit's smooth and body-molding lines. In January, 1950 Rose Marie Reid offered a swimsuit "sculptured to fit you."[6] The model in the suit kneels beside a small mirror which permits the text "Reflected Beauty..." Behind the model a sculpted figure in the identical pose rests on a column, with a Grecian urn in lieu of a mirror. The logo appearing at the bottom of the advertisement comprises a standing statue of Venus, also on a column, and the phrase The SCULPTURED swimsuit. Clearly the suit's sexy lines are to be emphasized by the association with Venus, its classic style by the column(s) and urn. The model, however, is no more animate than the statues which surround her, but is rather a drawing; perhaps Rose Marie Reid had a limited advertising budget, or, perhaps, the ad's creator thought it would be more evocative of the classical and its ideal to draw the perfectly sculpted figure rather than photograph a live woman.

COLE of California came out with a series of advertisements in 1970 that used a bust of Aphrodite to illustrate its swimsuits.[7] COLE presented the first of its

[5] The advertisement appeared, among other places, in *Vogue* (September, 1970).

[6] This advertisement appeared in *Vogue* (January, 1950).

[7] The series began in the October, 1970 issue of *Vogue*, and continued over the next several months.

Body Sculpture suits, naming the solid black onepiece "Michelangelo."[8] Model and sculpted bust turned toward each other, although (rather oddly) the bust turned its head away with an upturned hand blocking any view of the suit.

This sculpture, complete to the thighs, had been placed upon a column base. It was not an actual classical piece, however, for the breasts were strangely emphasized.[9] The "sculpture" had a rather pliant look, as if the figure was, indeed, a real woman, but with any real color removed by trick photography. COLE seemed to be making a double play on the words body sculpture: the "statue" was a woman photographed to look inanimate, the suit was so designed as to make its wearer be a work of art. This same "artifact" appeared in COLE's ads in the next few months, although in November and December the statue had its arms raised above its head, hands clasped, and the live model took the same position. November's colorful suit was named "Leonardo." The same sculpted figure appeared in December's advertisement, this time for a black suit with plunging bustline laced with white, a little number named "Phidias." Clearly the buyer of these rather pricey suits (c. $25. in 1970) was to think she was buying a true work of art, a creation worthy to be named after the world's greatest sculptors.

The COLE advertisements were some of the more risqué to appear in the magazines of 1970, setting a trend for the more sexually blatant illustrations of the following decades. COLE had caused a sensation as early as 1964 when the company came out with the suit named "Scandal." Modest by 1990s standards, the Scandal was the first with mesh inserts at the waist, allowing a peekaboo at the body's middle. The suit was promoted simply in 1964, allowing its style to do the provocation. Scandal sales brought COLE over $2 million, also earning the company a story on the front page of the Wall Street Journal.[10]

In 1975, a high-fashion advertisement presented Rudi Gernreich's "newest and barest bathing suit, the Thong"; it was promoted in a visually striking ad.[11] Clad

---

[8] Cole of California (founded by silent film actor Fred Cole in 1925) was the first company to bring body-clinging stretch fabric to swimwear. Anne Cole, daughter of the founder, started her own line of swimsuits in 1982.

[9] It was the oddly prominent breasts that made the figure look neither animate nor marble; these, indeed, disturbed the overall effectiveness of the illustration.

[10] Information on Cole of California and Anne Cole Collection from Margot Guralnick, "Anne Cole. America's swimsuit queen speaks out" (*Travel & Leisure*: July, 1998): 62-65.

[11] The advertisement appeared in *Vogue* (January, 1975) The photographer for this

in the brief swim-suits two women stand locked in a stance reminiscent of the chiastic figures of Greek vs. Centaur of the south metopes on the Parthenon. With her right hand on the waist of the other, the dark-haired woman seems to push her companion away, but with her left she grabs the other's blond hair and pulls her head back. The blond is thus forced into the pose of the Amazon on the shield of Athena Parthenos. Newton's image is powerful through its double invocation of familiar artistic portrayals of two myths very popular in Greek art and legend: the battles between Greeks and Centaurs, between Greeks and Amazons. The violence implicit in the advertisement is restrained by the art, also an echo of the Parthenon metopes and Athena's shield. The Thong ad certainly grabs attention, while its ambiguity arouses reflection: is the picture appropriate for the article in which it appears, a piece on keeping the skin protected from too much exposure to the sun (even when following the author's advice on the benefits of outdoor exercise)? By understanding the violence inherent in the mythology that informs the illustration, the dangers of overexposure to the sun may be recognized.

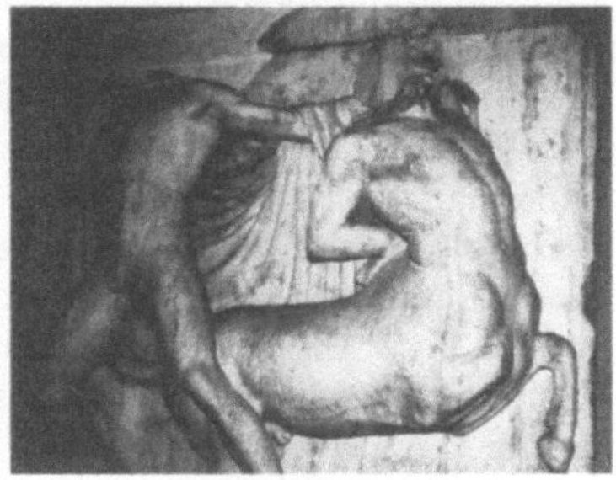

2.3 Centaur. Athens: Parthenon \ South Metope

The most popular of the ancient deities to enter the world of modern advertising was, as might be expected, Aphrodite, or Venus as the Romans called her. This goddess of sexual love came into being when Cronos castrated his father Ouranos and flung the cut off members into the sea; from the foam that gathered around these Aphrodite arose, ready to guide the passions of mortals. Such a deity is perfect for promoting women's attire, lotions, and perfumes. The variations on the love goddess for product promotion have been almost endless. The most obvious instances are those items which take their name directly from her name; everything from lingerie to linens, stockings to silverware, borrow her name or her image as created by ancient or Renaissance artists. The association of mortal with divinity immediately lifts the ordinary to a new realm of allure and power, and this realm, according to the men on Madison Avenue, is where the modern woman wants to be.

promotion was Helmut Newton, whose work is always on the edge of daring, as we will see later in his illustrations for some dresses of the 1990s.

The love-goddess became an appellation for lingerie and its manufacture. A Chicago-based underwear company took her name itself, while Goddess, a company in Cambridge, Massachusetts, marketed bras, "as lifting as love."[12] In 1950 A.H. Rogers & Company introduced a nightgown under the love goddess' name.[13] The advertisement shows a small line drawing of an (animated) classical statue in front of a live model wearing the gown. In another advertisement for the VENUS, the company presented its "newest, most talked of nightgown" on a (live) model relaxing on a chaise and talking on the telephone.[14] The gown with its "one shoulder dramatically bared" is described as "divinely comfortable." The text on the photograph is equally simple: "Speaking of Intimate Things..." Beside the description of the gown is drawn a classic statue, also in a long one-shoulder bared dress. Name, style, and illustration work well together in this advertisement: all women know the power of Venus and thus will want to buy this new gown. All women can afford it, too, for it cost about $4.00 and was available in either yellow or blue.

Barbizon also created a gown named for this goddess: in 1960, as part of its "Valentine Collection," the company presented its "Venus de Milo" gown in its "own pure satin de lys."[15] The demure dress was pictured on a live model whose hair was dressed in classic style and who held a golden apple in her left hand--no slipping robe on this model. Apparently the golden apple (long since vanished from almost all ancient statues) was to link name and dress, for there was nothing classical about the Barbizon gown "modeled by Michelle." A red curtain hung in columnar folds behind her; the white dress against the red drape emphasized the role it was to play for the February 14th holiday. The single eye-catching ad presented two romantic allusions: the goddess of love and love's holiday.

In April of 1950 F. Berlé printed a small ad based on classical allusion.[16] Next to a (labeled) photographed bust of Praxiteles' Aphrodite are printed block letters: bra relief. Picture and words play off our knowledge of ancient art (Praxitiles'

---

[12] This advertisement appeared, for example, in *Glamour* (March, 1950).

[13] The advertisement appeared in *Vogue* (March 15, 1950).

[14] This advertisement appeared (half-page)in *Glamour* (April, 1950) and (full page) in *Vogue* (March 15, 1950).

[15] The advertisement was published in *Vogue* (February 15, 1960).

[16] The advertisement was published in *Vogue* (April 15), 1950.

famous statue) and art vocabulary (bas-relief). The accompanying text has nothing to do with Aphrodite or art, however, but merely assures the buyer that a Delineator bra fits an individual's needs and has never, in 27 years, been successfully copied. It was an expensive bra, costing even in 1950 from $16.50 at fine stores. Perhaps the classic value of the bra rested in its price. Neither Berlé or its Delineator exist in today's market.

While many of the companies of the 1950s have vanished from the malls, one has remained a vital and strong competitor in the field of women's intimate apparel: Vanity Fair. In February, 1950, Vanity Fair Mills presented in *Vogue* a sheer gown, tied with a sash and coming with a matching peignoir, made of "peerless nylon tricot."[17] The gown was styled with a back bare to the waist, making it one of the earliest versions of what I call the Aphrodite-with-the-slipping-robe motif (see Chapter III). This bareback view of the model will become the standard for advertisements of all types in the ensuing decades.

In 1970 CATALINA, which "makes all your world a beach" offered an advertisement that was one of the first to suggest the Aphrodite-from-the-sea theme.[18] Presenting a simple turquoise two-piece bathing suit on a model kneeling at the wave's edge, the ad's text showed that the traditional Greek legend was playing in the mind of the ad's creator. Behind the model a faint image of her face filled the sky, against which was written:

> Water,
> whence I came and where I go,
> it sets me free.
> Cool and curved inside a wave
> uncurled inside my soul,
> I watch surflings lap around my knee,
> urging me.
> Can trouble go out on the tide?
> I think so, every city day.

While the closing lines of this free-form verse are clearly part of the contemporary world, the opening several couplets resound with mythic possibilities. While various sea nymphs (Thetis, mother of Achilles, Galatea, beloved of the Cyclops

---

[17] Its advertisement appeared in *Vogue* (February 15, 1950).

[18] The advertisement appeared in *Vogue* (November 15, 1970).

Polyphemus, or Amphitrite, wife of Poseidon, e.g.) could also claim to come and go from the sea, it was Aphrodite, born of the sea-foam and wafted ashore (either at Cytherea or Cyprus) whose epithets identified her as coming from the sea. As the goddess of sexual love, it was her power that would appeal to the creators of advertising, men and women who wanted sexuality to sell their product. From this simple illustration in 1970 was born a long tradition of women-and-the-sea pictures for contemporary advertising.

Maidenform made the most direct reference to the art of the love goddess. In an advertisement in its "I dreamed I was..." series, *maidenform* presented a model wearing its "Pre-Lude Once-Over" creation, draped with a slipping robe, claiming, "I dreamed I was Venus de Milo in my *maidenform* bra."[19] To anyone familiar with the statue or the mythology, the advertisement is an amusing blend of classical images. The "Venus of Melos" model, with her two beautiful arms outstretched, stands in the Parthenon (with Erechtheum behind for authenticity), leaning on a small copy of the "Praxiteles" Hermes (from Olympia). By bringing together several "classic" images never in reality so assembled, the layout designer apparently wanted to be sure the viewer understood this as an illustration based on The Greek Classics! The accompanying text reads, in part, "For the figure of the ages,....give your figure a touch of Venus." Ten years later *maidenform* returned to the theme but assumed its audience was familiar with the Aphrodite reference. For in this advertisement the model dreamed "I was a classic beauty."[20] The model, dressed in the new "Sweet Nothing" bra, wears her dark hair arranged in classic style and the slipping robe, and stands before the Temple of Neptune at Paestum. Despite the locale, we recognize that this is not just any "classic beauty" but the love goddess, and thus the advertisement maintains the power of this theme.

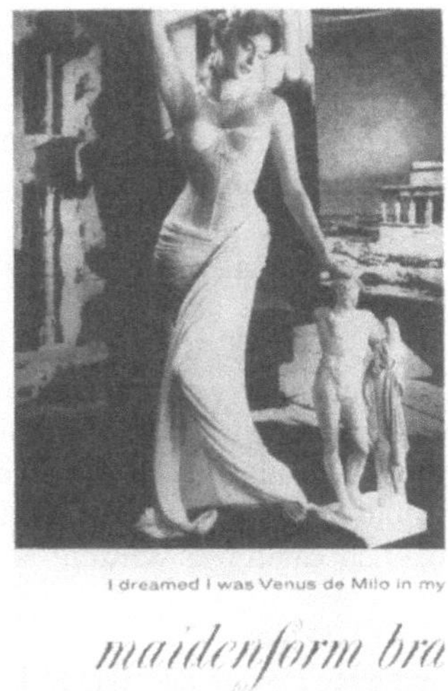

2.4 Maidenform: Bra

[19] The advertisement appeared, among other places, in *Vogue* (December, 1955).

[20] The advertisement appeared in many magazines, including *Vogue* (August, 1965).

Other Greek goddesses have lent their names to various articles of women's apparel: many bras, nightgowns, slips and swimsuits sport the names of the classical divinities. Artemis was the trademark for lingerie created by Weil-Kalter Manufacturing Company in the 1950s.[21] The garments sold under this name would seem to have little to do with the goddess of the hunt, who was never skimpily attired, and had little or nothing to do with things dainty and feminine. Nevertheless her name embroidered delicate women's wear for years.

Thus a 1950s ad presents in a gauzy full-page spread a drawing of a young woman in fancy party attire who opens a gift box, takes out a delicate slip and exclaims, "...and it's an Artemis!"[22] Stars sparkle around the image, on the gift box and its ribbons, and are repeated in the woman's earrings. The entire image seems directed toward the magical and thus appropriate for the name, for magic and myth are often closely associated.

Perfumes, Lotions, and Bath Oils

Many of the perfume advertisements have developed over the years from mere suggestions of mythological themes to clear expositions of the ancient images. The illustrations have become more explicit, too, with changing times. While many promotions for the various fragrances still picture just the bottle, many others present a model wearing (presumably) the scent, and some tell a story to sell their perfumes.

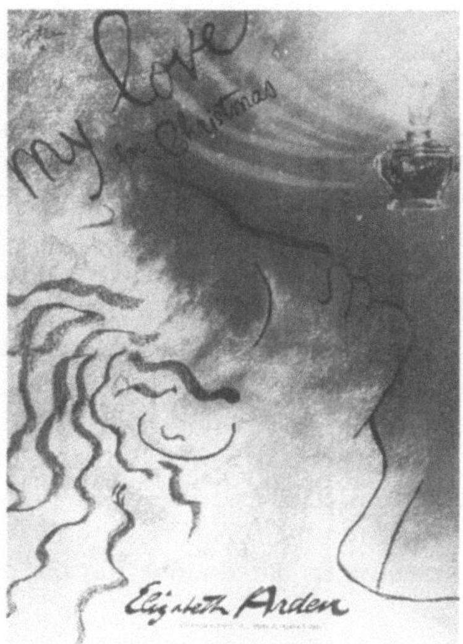

2.5 Elizabeth Arden: *My Love*

It was particularly fashionable in the 1950s and 1960s to advertise a product as used by a well-known person from the entertainment or high-society world:

[21]The company as an independent manufacturer has vanished; by 1970 it was Gossard-Artemis, and continuing the Artemis line.

[22] The advertisement appeared in *Vogue* (November 15, 1950).

movie stars or women known for their husband's name were often shown endorsing a particular scent or line of clothes.[23] Sometimes, however, the ad's creator would turn to figures from literature or art. Thus in December, 1950, just in time for Christmas, Elizabeth Arden brought out a new perfume called "My Love" and promoted it in the pages of *Vogue* and similar magazines with a Jean Cocteau drawing. The artfully shaped bottle was topped with a glass plume, a clever allusion to the French playwright, while the drawing was a typical Cocteau androgynous figure. Cocteau frequently cast his plays with figures from classical myth, e.g., Apollo in *Apollon du Belac* or Orpheus in the play titled from his name, and thus the perfume receives endorsement from thename, art and subject of Jean Cocteau's creations. Elizabeth Arden's perfume by its name alone would not stand out, but the initial advertisement brings it center stage: the educated shopper will remember that the French playwright drew his inspiration from the realm of classical myth, and thus the purchase of "My Love" will enhance its wearer in a special and enduring way.

Also in 1950, for his *Directoire* perfume Charles of the Ritz entered the lists of those creating advertisements based on the idea of classic. In a promotion appearing in magazines beginning in November, 1950, the perfume in its distinctive and classically shaped bottle was placed on a half column encircled with a vineleaf crown.[24] Across the column Charles assures us that this is "A distinctive perfume whose exquisite fragrance is carried through an entire ensemble." At the top of the full-page ad, a blue border set off a bevy of women attired in costumes of the 18th century. Above the framed picture was written: "Return to Elegance... To Splendour... To the Classic." Although the attire of the women is hardly ancient, the text, the column, and the wreath put forth the message clearly: *Directoire* is a fragrance with an impeccable reputation.

Allusions to Aphrodite or Venus appeared frequently in advertisements during the 1950s and 1960s. In 1955, Parfums WEIL came out with a perfume, "unlike any other perfume in the world," *Secret of Venus*. This scent rested its message on its name alone, for the model (apparently) wearing it is an ordinary

[23] It is worth noting that the women in these advertisements from the 1950s were known as wives, they were the creators of fine homes for their wealthy husbands. It is not until later that women who had made their own mark upon society were asked to put their imprimatur upon a given product.

[24] The advertisement appeared in *Vogue* (November 15, 1950).

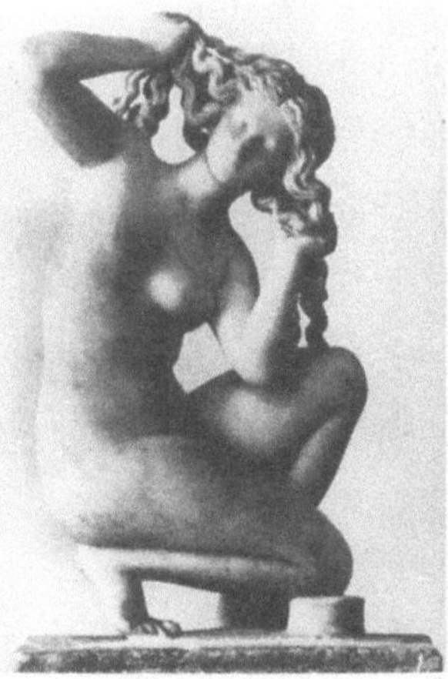

Left: 2.6
Aphrodite.
Rhodes \
Archaeological
Museum

Right: 2.7
Caron:
Perfume

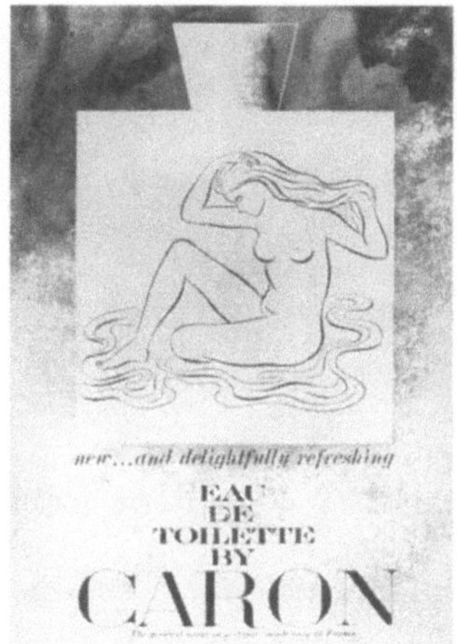

woman, and its bottle, while attractive, makes no classical allusion.[25] Name and image were linked, however, when CARON (the greatest name in perfume--made only in France) chose an echo of the Aphrodite Rising from the Sea as a generic illustration for all its fragrances.[26]The company offered a full-page ad in which water surrounds a nude female wringing her hair, an image that is within a square bottle that itself is surrounded by a frothy wave. The names of the various CARON perfumes run along the bottom of the page-and none of the names has anything to do with Aphrodite/Venus! The viewers of this advertisement are assumed to know the classical allusion and to realize that the effects of any CARON perfume will reflect that of the love-goddess, Aphrodite, whose gift to Paris Alexander (and presumably thus to others) was irresistible sex-appeal.

CARON was not alone in using this allusion. Dorothy Gray, in 1965 claimed [she] "did it!" It was "the Secret of the Sea." The creams and lotions were said to mystically draw and restore the skin's moisture to make a woman's skin soft and "breathtaking." The full-page illustration accompanying this announcement shows a nude woman emerging from the foam at the sea's edge, surely a direct echo of the

[25] The text of the ad notes that Parfums WEIL come in the three great fragrances, 'Zibeline,' 'Cassandra,' 'Antilope.' One of the names, Cassandra, is classical, but not a particularly auspicious name for a scent, while the other two names. Zibeline and Antilope, appear mythic but are not so.

[26] The advertisement appeared in *Vogue* (October (1960).

Birth of Venus shown in so many Renaissance paintings.[27] So it is not only the "secret of the sea" that we are supposed to associate with Dorothy Gray's new lotions but also the power of the love-goddess.

A nude woman not emerging but drifting in the waves was used as the promotion for Abano Bath Oil by Prince Matchabelli.[28] The text of this ad tells us that Abano "does just what the Ancients knew fragrance could do." After bathing in Abano, "you emerge, renewed for living." The idea of renewal gives a greater depth to the mythological implications of the advertisement. Renewal informs the legend of Hera's annual bath to renew her virginity; this adds a piquancy to the association. There are further ramifications of "re-newal," however, which the advertisement's creator might not have considered: the deity that is renewed, reborn, is believed to have died before rebirth. Even Persephone, daughter of Demeter, must return to the realm of the dead every fall before she can emerge each spring. But the allusion to the sea-goddess/love goddess springs first to mind, so the total effect of the advertisement is positive.

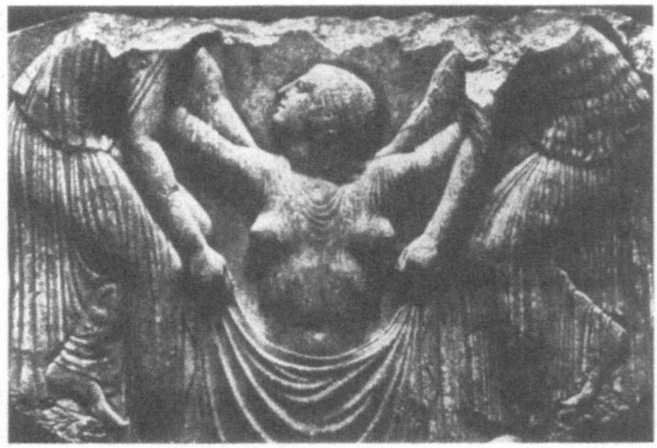

2.8 Hera. Ludovisi Throne. Rome \ Museo Nationale

Over the years Monteil has promoted several fragrances with advertisements based on classical myth.[29] In 1950 Germaine Monteil introduced two new perfumes and presented them in a single advertisement (itself a rather unusual step, although other perfumes did so from time to time, e.g., Dana, when showing its complete line

[27] The advertisement appeared in *Vogue* (Novebmer, 1965). This image will become one of the most popular tropes in the advertisements of the 1990s (see Chapter III).

[28] The advertisement appeared in *Vogue* (December, 1965).

[29] Monteil has changed ownership several times and changed its name as well: Germaine Monteil and Monteil Paris are two; the company is now owned by Coty (and Monteil products no longer sold in the United States).

of scents). *Laughter* and *Nostalgia* were advertised with an illustration derived from the ancient Greek world.[30] A colored line drawing showed a woman in evening attire seated on park steps and apparently entranced by a very debonair satyr. Only three words, in tiny print, appeared on the page other than the names of the fragrances and their manufacturer: "two exciting perfumes." Although ancient satyrs were not always the best of company, in this advertisement the goatish figure is a delightful source of laughter, while his very appearance from classical Arcadia brings a sense of nostalgia. The illustration is visually arresting, but the echoes it initiates are not entirely pleasing, its ambiguity rather unsettling. Will the wearer of either fragrance find excitement in the liminal world of mythic satyrs? As with the Perry Ellis ads of the 1990s for instance (see Chapter V), a woman might think twice before purchasing either *Laughter* or *Nostalgia*.

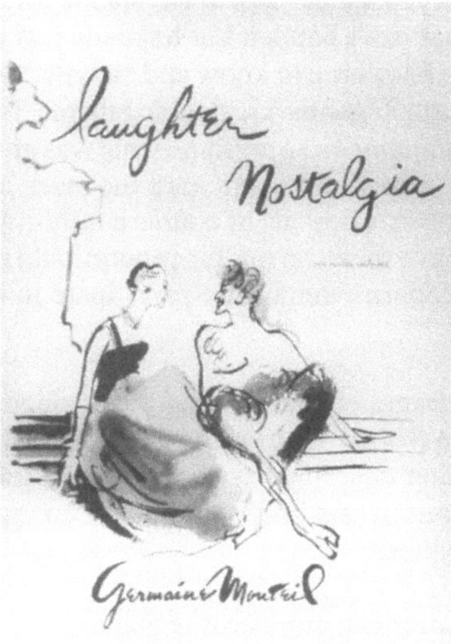

2.9 Monteil: *Laughter & Nostalgia*

Monteil kept the classic theme to promote its *Royal Secret* bath perfume in 1960. This time the ad, still in line drawing, was based strictly on Grecian art.[31] Over the text "For that feeling of utter luxury" stood a woman in a peplos-style dress, pouring liquid from an amphora over a nude female kneeling in an Aphrodite-from-the-sea position. The name of the bath perfume has nothing to do with Greece, but the illustration adds further class to *Royal Secret*.

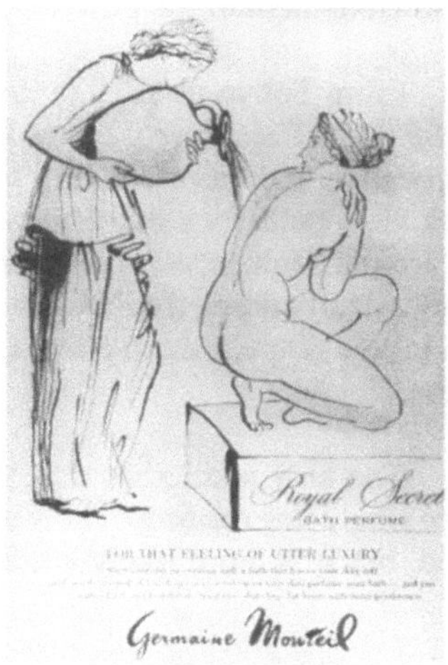

2.10 Monteil: *Royal Secret*

[30] In an advertisement in *Vogue* of 1 April, 1950.

[31] This advertisement was published in *Vogue* (February, 1960).

To promote its fragrances of the 1970s, Guerlain created mini-stories for each of its aromas: the company asserted that each of its designer bottles "holds a story even before it holds a drop of perfume."[32] To enhance this rather unusual statement, the company did indeed tell a tale for each of its fragrances; *Chant'd'Arômes*, for example "tells the story of a time when lovers used the flowers of the field to carry messages they were too shy to speak,"*Mitsouko* stands for an unhappy love affair, "the story of any love that can't happen but happens just the same," while *Shalimar*'s story is one everyone has come to know and "is true."*Vol de Nuit* and *L'Heure Bleue* also had romantic legends created for them. The possibilities for a series of illustrations to accompany these perfume vials was great, but in 1970 Guerlain was content to have its potential buyers read the story and imagine the figures suggested. Each of the little "stories" is, of course a mini-myth (even *Shalimar*'s "true tale" might be said to have taken on mythic proportions) and it is by wearing Guerlain's perfumes that a modern woman can participate in the romantic legends the scents are said to evoke.

In the 1970s Fabergé came out with a fragrance the company described as "Perhaps the most aptly named fragrance in the world": *Aphrodisia*.[33] Packaged in a simple columnar bottle, the perfume was further described as "Fragrance of love. Mysterious. Unmistakable. An unspoken but irresistible summons," an open acknowledgment of the power of the love-goddess.

From Tokyo in 1970 to the finest of American stores came Hannae Mori's SHISEIDO. The advertisement appearing in the September issue of *Vogue* was provocative and an interesting blend of eastern and western imagery. A model (back view), clearly a western woman, nude but for a golden chain multi-stranded belt around her hips, was the central image; a single strand of her dark hair fell from her classically dressed coiffure and curled in thecenter of her back. She was seated on a billow of black cloth printed in white with what were to appear to be Japanese letters.

The only text, other than the company's name and the cost of the perfume was a single line reading "The Very Breath of Love." The billow of cloth might be a cloud, but it is more likely a wave, and the figure rising from it could easily be

---

[32] These advertisements began appearing in *Vogue* and other magazines beginning in April, 1970.

[33] It was advertised thus *Glamour* (June, 1975).

Aphrodite. The golden chain-belt, meanwhile, recalls that worn by the love-goddess and borrowed by Hera (*Iliad* XIV.214 ff), the intricate accessory adorning the familiar statue of Aphrodite found at Ostia. Here, then, is one of the first illustrations to take its inspiration from this myth which would become so very popular in the early 1990s, a myth which would be used primarily for perfume advertisements but equally employed to promote products ranging from cars to shampoos to handbags.

The love-goddess was not the only divinity whose power was reflected in perfume advertisements. Dionysus, god of nature, of emotion-- and wine -- has also played a role in product promotions; an analysis of his influence on print media ads may be found in Chapter III. An early advertisement that appears to express Dionysiac freedom was created by Chanel in 1975, when the company suggested its perfumes and cosmetics created "another feeling."[34] In this advertisement (illustrated in Chapter III) the model for Chanel *N° 19* was pictured in mid-swirl while her expression remained cool and calm. Her appearance reflects the nature of Dionysus as Euripides' describes him in *The Bacchae*: calm and detached while creating ecstasy. The model's cool look would remain part of Chanel's illustrations over the years; the emotion the 1975 advertisement for *N° 19* suggests served to introduce an idea of Dionysian power that remained a part of Chanel's advertising campaigns.

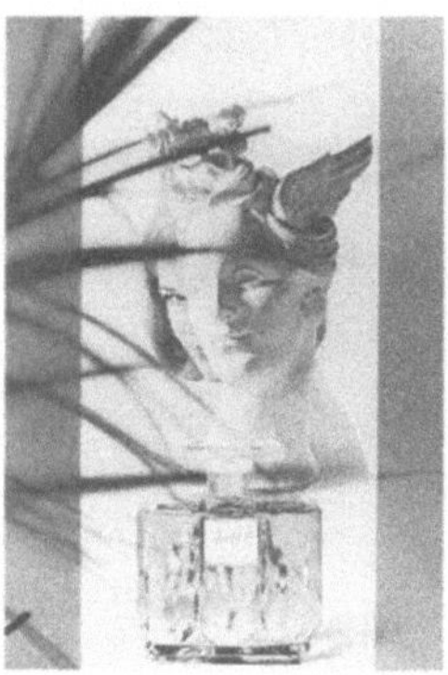
2.11 Dana: *Ambush*

In the mid 1960s Dana offered a new perfume unusual in name, motto, and art. The name selected for this scent is *Ambush,* a name that tells us little but suggests a lot. We can surmise that the wearer takes those who approach her by surprise; those she seeks are captured unsuspectingly by the aroma. The motto, however, adds a further and interesting dimension: "from the goddess of fragrance... *Ambush* perfume." What does this mean? Is Dana the goddess of fragrance? Or has the creator of the scent been guided by this divinity? (One does not ask who or which divinity this might be; it is clearly not one of the regular pantheon of gods.) Whence comes this aroma? The mystery remains.

[34] The advertisement appeared, e.g., in *Vogue* (March, 1975).

The artwork chosen to advertise this perfume is equally intriguing, equally ambiguous, although it does seem to reflect the name, and possibly the motto.[35] A classical head is portrayed behind the tri-form bottle, but a head unlike any existing statue of a deity. While the visage is very like that of Apollo, the features are more feminine and thus this is surely the goddess of fragrance. But she has appropriated for herself wings such as those on the hat of Hermes /Mercury, while centered on her head is a cap of flowers, vaguely reminiscent of the poppies crowning the Minoan goddesses. Thus we have before us the goddess of fragrance. Peering out from behind the statue is a woman, clearly in ambush; she smiles knowingly from her partial hiding place. A spray of fronds shadows both heads; goddess and her accomplice are lying in wait for their prey. Again we have no idea what aroma *Ambush* might offer, but we are certain that it is one that will arouse old memories; while these memories are flitting by, the one held by the scent will be taken by its wearer. The woman who chooses *Ambush* is now a powerful hunter: divinity and perfume give her power.

It is instructive to trace the history of the promotions of a given product, how it has been advertised over the past 30-40 years. Many of the perfume advertisements have developed from mere suggestions of mythological themes to clear expositions of the ancient images. The illustrations have become more explicit, too, as times and morals changed. While many promotions for the various fragrances still picture just the bottle, many others present a model (presumably) wearing the scent, and some tell a story to sell their perfumes. Three companies, Evyan, Dana and Coty, have consistently turned to a classical trope to promote their fragrances, Greek myth has underscored their advertisements, sometimes quite openly, sometimes in subtle suggestion. Either way, the viewer's assumed familiarity with ancient legend heightens the message of the advertisements.

Evyan's White Shoulders

A perfume which has endured for many years is Evyan's *White Shoulders*. In the 1950s, a picture of the bottle itself was enough to capture the buyer's attention. For its summer "Splash" fragrance, Evyan placed the crystal topped bottle beside a breaking wave; tiny print assured its wearer the "Splash" would make the skin satin, highlight the hair and be refreshing in the summer's heat. In another

---

[35] The advertisements appeared in color in *e.g. Glamour* (September, 1964 through April, 1965), as well as in pure white e.g., *Glamour (*May, 1965); the white advertisement promoted spray colognes in general, with the tag line "the goddess symbol that is Dana."

advertisement of the 1950s, "Splash" was illustrated with a mermaid opening a treasure chest beneath the sea.[36]

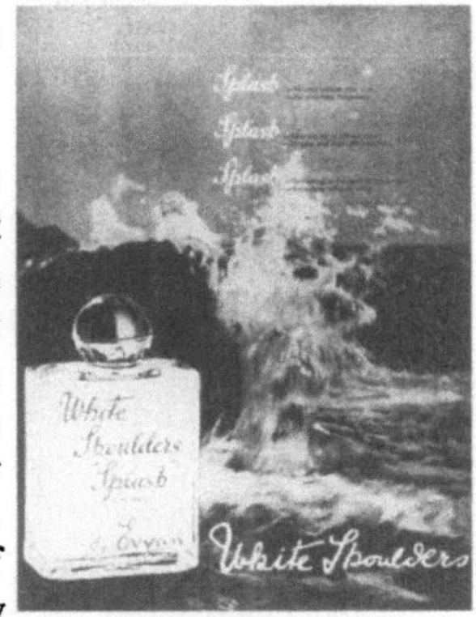

2.12 Evyan: *Splash*

Twenty years later, Evyan had turned to sex appeal to sell this perfume. In a striking advertisement appearing in magazines in 1970, we are looking down on the face and shoulders of a model whose dark hair spreads out around her, whose eyes are closed in ecstasy.[37] Her ivory-like face and shoulders dominate the picture, but a closer look reveals the source of her delight, as we notice a man's head against her breast. No text accompanied the image, only a small picture of the vial and the simple statement of name and company stands in the border at the top of the page. Passion has entered perfume advertising. The woman who wears *White Shoulders* will experience the intense emotion of the model, but emotion revealed through her pose not her expression: her face is as idealized as that of any classical Greek statue. While no immediate myth lies behind this ad, its suggested classicism rests upon its similarity to classical sculpture. But it does suggest a story, and from a story it is but a short step to myth.

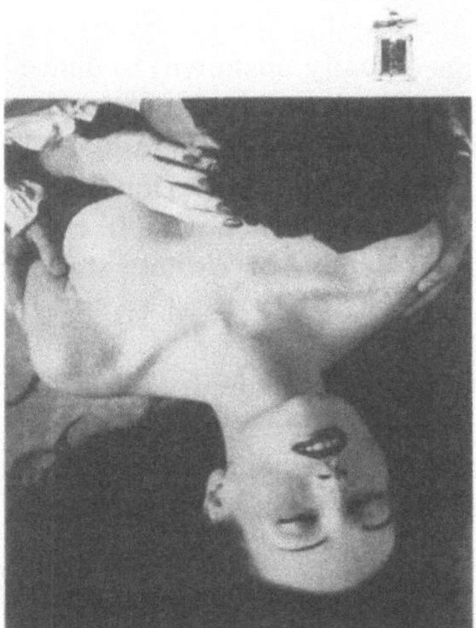
2.13 Evyan: *White Shoulders*

Five years later Evyan left nothing to mere suggestion. In its advertisements for *White Shoulders* (whose vial had been altered from a simple rectangle to an emphasized square), Evyan's model was much more demure than the passionate

[36] The bottle by the wave advertisement appeared in *Vogue* (May 15, 1950); the mermaid advertisement in *Glamour* (June, 1950).

[37] This advertisement appeared widely, including in *Vogue* (November 15, 1970).

woman of the 1970 advertisement.[38] Here she looks at us over her bare white shoulder, a handsome man in evening dress appears behind her. Surrounding her is a cluster of women in various states of deshabille. At the bottom of the page we are told: "Background: Ladies in waiting to Empress Eugenie. Winterhalter Painting from the Royal Collection. Buckingham Palace, London." Yes, but these ladies in waiting were never truly in attendance upon Empress Eugenie; they are figures of classical myth, of the sort we see in illustrations of Venus and Adonis, if not in more lascivious scenes of nymphs and Satyrs. Implied sexuality is as much a part of this advertisement as it was of the more explicit illustration of 1970. This model may be demure, but her challenging glance and the figures which surround her clearly indicate that passion is near. The woman who chooses *White Shoulders* will enjoy romance soon.

In *Promotional Culture*, Andrew Wernick points out, in his discussion of how contemporary advertising has had to (re-) image male gender, that in the 1950s the male model, like the female, was always assumed to be a family man. That expectation vanished in the 1970s in favor of romance. He writes:

> The fantasy male waiting in the wings (usually unshown) to dance attendance on the wearer of Givenchy or Charles of the Ritz could be her actual husband. But he could also be her pre-or extra-marital lover. And in this exotic stranger (Prince Charming? Don Juan? Napoleon?) there is more than a trace of the Bad Man who, like the Bad Woman, has long been an important element of Western sexual mythology.[39]

The *White Shoulders* advertisement promotes new roles for both women and men in the consumer world of the 1970s, and by its very nature helps define what those new roles are to be. Advertising responds to culturaldemands and expectations, it also serves to shape them. Passion arrives via perfume, perfume attracts by its association with the goddess of passion.

---

[38] This advertisement also appeared widely, including in the pages of *Vogue* (May, 1975).

[39] Andrew Wernick, *Promotional Culture. Advertising, ideology and symbolic expression.* (London: Sage Publications: 1991): 51.

DANA's *TABU*

Aphrodite mythology has subsets as well, and one of the best known is that of Pygmalion, the artist who falls in love with his work and whose work becomes animate through the agency to the love goddess. Pygmalion, a young sculptor on the island of Cyprus, had become disgusted with the women of his island, all of them prostitutes as a result of Aphrodite's anger; he thus carved a statue of his ideal woman. So much time did he spend with her that he soon wished she could be more than a cold statue, that she could become his animate beloved. He prayed to Aphrodite for this and she answered theprayer of the devout young man. Thus did his statue, sometimes named Galatea, become a real and loving woman, and Pygmalion became the paradigm for the artist who falls in love with his work. George Bernard Shaw immortalized the legend for western audiences with his 1916 play named for the artist, while in 1956 Alan Jay Lerner and Frederick Loewe made the story one of the best known musicals of all time with*My Fair Lady*, playing both on Broadway and later on the silver screen. The old play and movie, *One Touch of Venus* also tells the story,[40] while the recent cinema box office hit, *Pretty Woman*, transformed Richard Gere and Julia Roberts into Pygmalion and his beautiful creation.[41]

The artist swept off his feet with passion for the woman wearing TABU is an idea Dana has used for years in its advertisements for the perfume. The company has long played off the name of its popular fragrance: for the wearer of TABU, the taboo is not forbidden, the illicit experience is possible and even, perhaps, permissible. One might expect that the interest would rest upon what lies within the restricted realm of

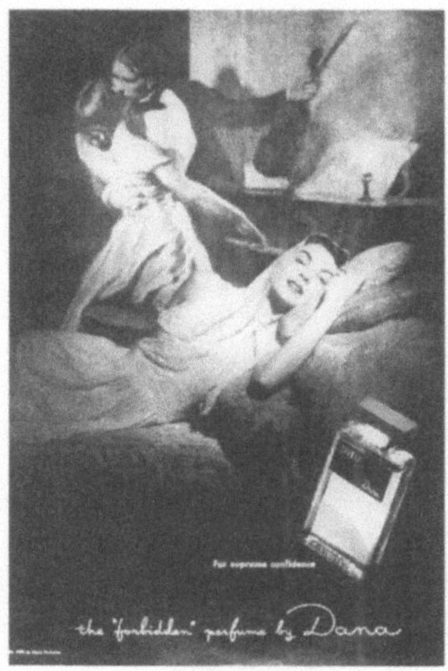

2.14 Dana: *Tabu*, 1950

---

[40] *One Touch of Venus*: screenplay by Harry Kurnitz and Frank Tashliln, with score by Kurt Weill, starred Ava Gardner and Robert Walker under the direction of William A. Seiter (1948).

[41] *Pretty Woman*: directed by Gary Marshall, credited writing by J. F. Lawton, 1990.

action, whether this changes in the course of time. A review of Dana's advertisements, however, reveals something rather different.

In the 1950s, Dana's advertisements portrayed a woman daydreaming of romance. For example, in April, 1950, the ad pictures a woman reclining on a daybed or chaise, attired in a soft evening gown.[42] The misty image of her dreams appears behind her: a violinist suddenly taking his pianist inan impassioned and spontaneous embrace. The taboo event is presented at one remove, for we are shown not the dream of the artist but that of his subject. For we must assume the pianist and the model are the same, the outcome of wearing TABU is her desire,not his; Dana wants women to buy its perfume. At most we can wonder whether the forbidden moment fills her dreams as an event that has happened or one she wishes would occur. Two lines of text appear in the lower part of the page; beside the picture of the traditional squared bottle is printed "For supreme confidence," while across the bottom of the picture runs in italics "the 'forbidden' perfume by Dana," the company's standard promotional phrase.

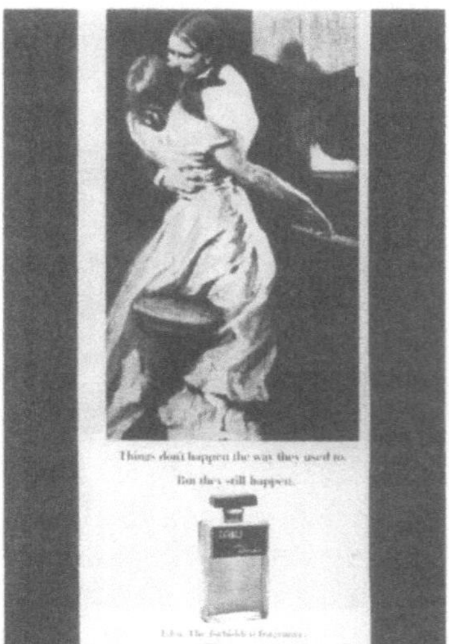

2.15 Dana: *Tabu,* 1970

Twenty years later Dana was using exactly the same image. In June, 1970, Dana presented the same man, the same woman at the piano--neither had aged a bit in the passing years![43] This time the text appears to play into the tradition: "Things don't happen the way they used to. But they still happen." What does this mean? According to the visual of this advertisement, "Things" do happen exactly as they used to. The careful observer of Dana's advertising campaign, the dedicated buyer of this perfume, can rest assured that while the world may turn and change, this fragrance remains provocative. By the end of 1970, Dana was playing up the long-lasting appeal of this fragrance.

[42] This advertisement appeared widely, including in the pages of *Vogue* (April 1, 1950).

[43] The advertisement appeared, for example, in *Vogue* (June, 1970).

The text accompanying the man and woman read, "If you want to inspire something lasting, do it with something that lasts," and, below the bottle, "Tabu. The lasting fragrance." As the visual image persists, so does the effect of the perfume.

Even five years later, in 1975, Dana repeated the same two figures. Still the man sweeps the pianist into his arms, still she is caught in his embrace. The text provides the meaning: "When you get this far into Tabu, there's no turning back." Dana took an interesting approach to its advertising: the image had become as recognizable as the name and, presumably, the aroma. But Dana was risking the possibility that the familiar can become the unnoticed. As the company had not really created names or a story for these two people, they did not become part of the VI/P figures of advertising.[44] The Visual Image/Personalities, such as, e.g., Pillsbury Doughboy, 9 Lives' Morris, and Rice Krispies' "Snap, Crackle, Pop" brought a different kind of life to name recognition. While clearly Dana might not want the humor of these particular figures, and is interested in print ads, not TV spots, still identifiable persons, real or created, can only help a product's popularity, as, for instance, Robert Morley for British Airways, or Jesse White for Maytag. Dana's musicians and their passion remained anonymous; the advantage of this anonymity was that they could be the subject of any woman's dream.

Thus the realm of the TABU did not change: the violinist swept off his feet by passion for his pianist continued to illustrate the seductive danger of wearing this fragrance. One might ask, however, if a relationship between these two musicians is still illicit? We know nothing about them except that their attraction has been long lasting! It will be several more years before Dana turns to a new theme.

Finally in 1995 a new illustration appeared.[45] The idea of sudden passion remained, but a different meaning was imputed to the embrace. So that the new image would be immediately understood, Dana's ad agency maintained the ancient myth. But gone are the refinements of the earlier advertisement. In the new Dana ad the Pygmalion story was told with a twist: the artist is female and the work of art male. This alteration offered an interesting variation in the realm of role reversal and equal rights, implying that women have become part of, or even taken over, not only masculine areas of the real world but also of the mythological realm.

---

[44] See Harry Wayne McMahan, "Do your ads have VI/P?" *Advertising Age* (July 14, 1980): 50-52.

[45] Advertisement appeared in many magazines, including *Mademoiselle* (November, 1995) and *Cosmopolitan* (November, 1995).

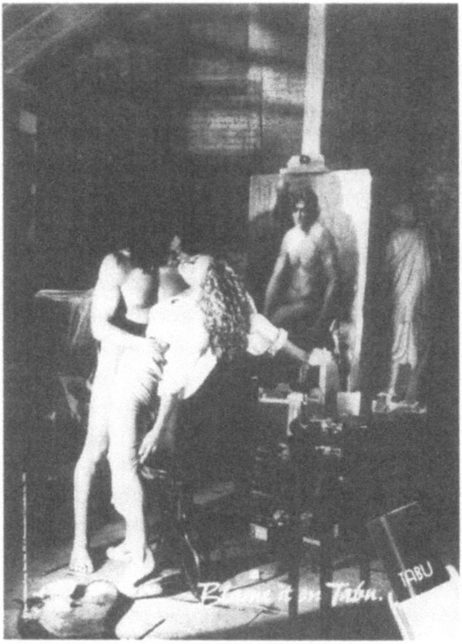

2.16 Dana *Tabu*, 1995

In a dark attic studio, with a classic statue of Diana standing forgotten in the shadows, a very modern woman has been painting a handsome male nude. The nearly complete canvas is on her easel. Suddenly the model leaps from his pose and embraces the artist; she drops her palate and brush and seems to be swooning in his arms. The illustration catches the two at the moment just before the subject kisses his creator. The ad's text reads, "Blame it on Tabu."

Although the model's image remains on the canvas, his very real self dominates the ad's picture as well as the woman. The Pygmalion legend dominates the advertisement. The darkened room, the classical statue recall the classical world, while the woman's complete surrender suggest it was she who was first in love with her work. She did not call upon Aphrodite to answer her desires, however, but relied upon the power of her perfume. TABU brought her lover to life, responsibility for this scene rests with its fragrance.

We cannot know what there is about TABU's scent that can bring art to life. We can know, however, that it has the power to do so, to transgress nature's bounds, the power to bring secret longings to reality. Dana had found a potent new image to promote its popular perfume.

Coty Perfume

Coty has a long history of the use of classical myth in the names of its fragrances and its advertisements for them.[46] As early as 1905 Coty turned to the

[46] This information on Coty's family of historic fragrances was sent (unsolicited) to me by Rick Kinsel, Director of Curatorial Services at Coty. I am deeply indebted to him for his assistance on this project.

classical for inspiration: *Ambre Antique* was packaged in a golden vial embossed with a circle of beautiful Grecian women.[47] The standing figures recalled the seated muses well-known from many a Greek vase, recalled also the popular Tanagra figures, statuettes of women in the attire of the period.

The Muse was herself the inspiration for a new perfume launched in 1946. Called *Muse*, the fragrance took "eight years of subtle, masterful blending of more than thirty ingredients." In its first promotion the text proclaimed that Muse "is destined to become a classic." One of Coty's full page ads was bordered with the Greek meander and a series of line-drawings of women dressed in classical attire, others allowed women, drawn in colorful evening attire vaguely reminiscent of ancient style to stand as the central image. These women, wearing Muse and thus "sharing the secrets of the goddesses," were the link between the classical world to which the Muses belong and the modern world where women wear Coty's newest creation.

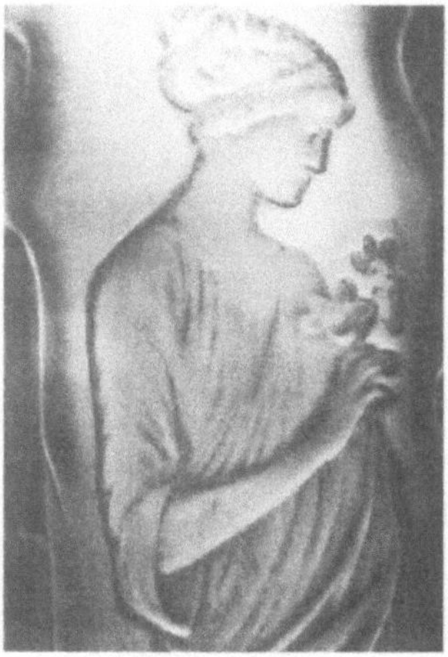
2.17 Coty: *Ambre*

Under the auspices of Coty in the 1980s, a new figure appeared in the world of fashion fragrances. Nikos Apostolopoulos, who had made his name in designing underwear and bathing suits in high tech fabrics sleekly cut for men and women, turned to creating perfumes. Under a winged lion logo, Nikos Parfums reflected both French and Greek worlds. Nikos had built his reputation in Paris, but his inspiration came from his Hellenic roots. The full page advertisements for his perfumes are texts, texts that tell his story or the story of a scent's name. In describing his creation one ad read:

> Nikos' creations are almost scientific in the sence (sic) that they draw on Greek geometry and feel for proportion, but they are also spiritual because they glorify the human body as a perfect mythological form. Like neoclassical architecture, they are historical in their inspiration, but utterly modern in their philosophy, transcendental and timeless.[48]

[47] The illustration for this advertisement was sent to me by Richard Kinsel.

[48] Nikos of 1994, a 14-page series of advertisements sent to me by Rick Kinsel, Coty's

Nikos titled one of his new perfumes "Sculpture" (to be pronounced in French) and its promotional text affirmed two levels of meaning: the lion in stone and his own creations which "shape the body into art through the strength of design." The scent was a blending of ancient and modern. But the text which described how the perfume got its name rivals a recollected dream. The beauty of a marble sculpture overwhelmed Nikos; he saw its lifeless eyes brought to life by the light reflecting off a glass amphora in the statue's hand. From that amphora a drop of perfume, a scent of jasmine and laurel, seemed to create "a moment of eternity." Thus Nikos named his fragrance "Sculpture: the Elixir of Life." All of the advertisement texts were enhanced or shadowed with classical sculpture or columns. In the Nikos promotions and products, name, creator, text and illustration formed a unified whole, and that whole sprang from the classical Greece in which was rooted Nikos Apostolopoulos' heritage and came to life under the guidance of Coty.

THREE GRACES

Three is a magical number. In ancient myth the Horae or Seasons were three, the Graiai or Personifications of Old Age were three, the Gorgons were three, soon even Moira, Fate, was divided into three: Clotho, Lachesis and Atropos. Three goddesses vied in contest for the most beautiful as designated by the apple of Eris, Goddess of Discord: Hera, Athena and Aphrodite requested that Paris determine which of them was most fair. The trio most often represented in ancient art was that of the three Charites or Graces. The popularity of their representations was clear, for their number permitted the artist to create three lovely ladies, and thus numerous vase paintings portray the three Graces. When the artists of the Renaissance discovered the classical world, one of their most popular subjects was again the three Graces; the maidens appealed to the post-classical artists in the same way as they attracted the ancient.

This preference for three women holds true for contemporary advertising as well. Time after time the advertising artist has chosen to represent a trio to promote the product. While that product is often clothing, and thus three styles can be shown in one page of advertisement, frequently the trio's attire is not particularly different. It is the power of three that captures the viewer's attention. This preference for the trio remains consistent throughout the period of this study; we find examples from

---

Director of Curatorial Services. The exact meaning of this text seems rather obscure, but its intent is clear: to evoke the spirit of ancient Greece as an inspiration for a Nikos parfum.

the 1950s to the present. Whether the ad is a line drawing or a photograph, three women are presented. Sometimes they stand almost in isolation looking out at the viewer, sometimes they seem to be interacting. In looking at them we are at times taken into their secret, but at other times it seems we are interlopers at their game. The former will attract us to buy the product and so become one of the inner circle, the latter will have the same effect: perhaps if we buy this we, too, can become part of that alluring secret. When the trio is presented as three independent women, it is as if each challenges the viewer to make the distinction, to be able to make a distinct choice. Each triad representation is a clever ploy on the part of the advertising artist, for each arouses the buyer's interest in a different way, yet it is the fact that there are three women, not one, that immediately attracts the viewer's attention.

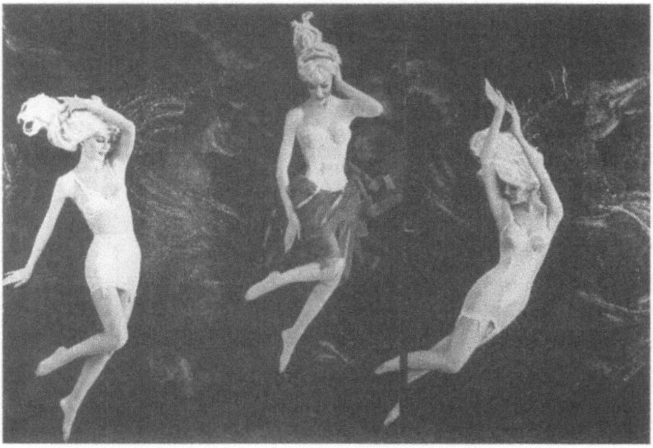

2.18 Warner: Girdles

Hats, coats, dresses, uniforms, blouses (especially blouses), bathing suits, and lingerie are all offered to the shopper in units of three. Schiaparelli, in an ad appearing in *Glamour* of August, 1950, presented four fragrances— illustrated with a line drawing of three figures taken (more or less) from classical vase paintings. In May, 1960 Warners ran this two-page ad for its various girdles and corselets.[49] The text plays to the mythic allusion: "No myth the way Warner's brings out the sylph in you...Three lace-ful ways to a fabled figure...your look for...spring eternal."

[49] The advertisement appeared in *Vogue* (May, 1960).

Rose Marie Reid portrayed her new line of dresses as "Swimshapes al Greco" in a two-page ad in the January, 1960 *Vogue*. The text underscores the style: "Rose Marie Reid sculpts... for your figure as though modeling swimsuits in alabaster... Behold the lyrical lines [of] Dorica, fluted with cummerbund, Theta neo-classic sheath, Medea, permanently pleated Arnel® swimdress." Dorica's fluting is appropriate, but the mythologically aware shopper might hesitate before Medea's pleats: Medea is the barbarian queen who slew her own children to punish her straying husband.[50]

GIANNI VERSACE advertisements are permeated with myth: his clothing sales campaigns will appear throughout this study; even his logo comes from the ancient world. Thus he frequently turns to the Three Graces as subject for his advertisements. In one of his finest illustrations (appearing in November, 1995) VERSACE shows three models in sequined gowns, in gold, blue, and silver, each with a different neckline, swept together into a single form. VERSACE's models often appear in contorted poses and these three are no exception, but the final tableau is pleasing and shows off the gowns well.[51]

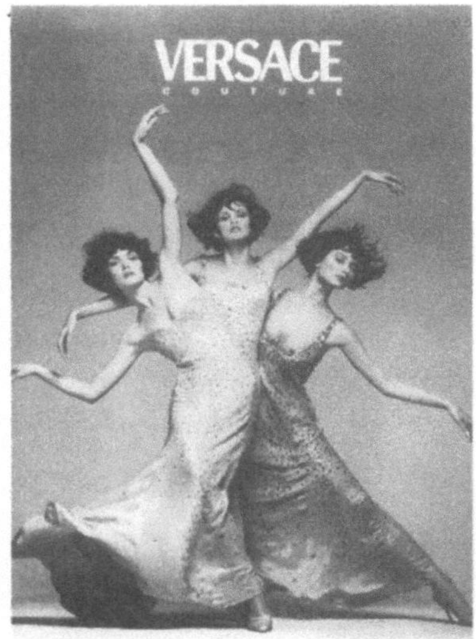

2.19 Gianni Versace: Gowns

So the trilogies are consistent. The threes are usually ofwomen, we must

[50] Sometimes even Three Graces advertisements miss the mark. In 1960, Triumph of Europe, Inc., in advertising its "Distinction" corselet, seems to have lost the meaning of triadic power. In an ad appearing in *Vogue* (September, 1960) the model stands apart from a triad of women. The text asserts that Europe's "Distinction" "gives you a figure so beautiful...other women will hate you!" The three women are pouring the model a poison cocktail. How can this advertisement be read in a positive way? The model attired in her "Distinction" is about to be poisoned by the united actions of three women in red. Despite the placement of the figure we are supposed to favor the odds are against her, for three women, whether gentle as the Graces or bristling as the Gorgons, will in the long run win the day.

[51] This advertisement appeared in all popular magazines in November, 1995, including *Glamour* and *Marie Claire*.

note; men stand alone or in duos.[52] Thus it seems that while the power of three is magical, it the three Graces that dominate the field in classical allusion.

In these pages, then, I have traced the history of several promotional campaigns from the 1950s to the 1990s, and have shown how ancient myth played a role in the print media advertisements during these forty years. But it is in the last decade of the 20th century that myth has become a major source of inspiration for those who work "on Madison Avenue." It is time to turn to the advertisements of the 1990s and consider how the Muse has guided the hands and thoughts of those creating advertising copy for this period.

---

[52]Jordache jeans broke the pattern in its May 1995 promotion, showing a mixed trio: one woman (blond), one black man, one white man (dark-haired). Jeans advertisements, as shown throughout this study, are often on the edges of the expected.

III
DOMINANT FIGURES OF MYTH IN ADVERTISEMENTS

From among the many figures of ancient myth, certain figures have appeared more often than others in product promotions, certain legends attracted more frequent attention. On the heights of Mt. Olympus dwelt at least twelve divinities who looked down on the doings of mortals, guiding their actions, rewarding them, punishing them or intervening according to some divine purpose or whim. These gods held sway over various aspects of human life, serving (perhaps) as the personifications of mortal passions, controlling the blessings and destructions of nature, certainly taking an interest in the interactions of men and women within either the bonds of family or the obligations of society. From time to time, according to legend, the divinities would appear among mortals, usually in a disguise that would suddenly vanish when it was appropriate for mortals to know a god was among them.

The ancient deities have continued to appear in the modern world in art, film, literature and, as this study makes clear, in advertising. The greater majority of the divine epiphanies in print media ads is in the promotions for women's attire and perfume. Their appearance with these articles is not surprising, since the beautiful divinities of the ancient pantheon naturally add allure to a woman's attire and toilette. But the ancient gods are used to promote a wide variety of products, as we shall see here and in the following chapter.

Of this Greek pantheon, of the 12 deities who ruled from Mt. Olympus, four deities reign supreme in the world of modern advertising: Zeus, Dionysus, Apollo and, especially, Aphrodite. This chapter sets out how these particular gods have appeared in print media advertisements during the 1990s.

ZEUS

Zeus, king of the gods, most powerful of the divinities, looked after those aspects of society that best held it together. He was the guarantor of oaths, he saw that host and guest showed each other proper and honest treatment, he guided the consummation of marriage, he offered salvation to those in dire need. He expressed his anger with thunderbolts, showed his approval with lightning, and took delight when men showed him honor through athletic pursuits at the Olympic and Nemean games. Zeus oversaw man's vaunting display of physical prowess and the moral structure of social interaction.

Nevertheless there were times when he followed his whims and took an active sexual interest in mortal maidens. While each of his affairs can be seen as part of a larger picture of creation and origin, the stories themselves offered entertainment to those who heard them and an attractive subject matter for artists working on vases, frescoes or mosaics in the ancient world and in more modern media in post-classical times. And it is these stories about Zeus and his various liaisons that have attracted the attention of the modern advertiser as well. Among the many females who attracted the attention of Zeus and who appear in contemporary advertisements are Danaë, Europa, and Leda.

Although the myth of Danaë has considerable potential for contemporary perfume advertisements, its appearance in the print media has been rather rare. According to the ancient legend, an oracle told the king of Argos that he was destined to die at the hands of his grandson. To avert this fate, Acrisius imprisoned Danaë, his only daughter, in a bronze-lined rocky cavern. But Zeus thwarted his intent to keep his daughter pure and penetrated her enclosure as a shower of golden rain. Classical and Renaissance painters portray the maiden welcoming the refreshing drops with outstretched limbs, a delicate yet suggestive interpretation of this divine impregnation. It is from this "union" that Perseus is born, Perseus who will decapitate Medusa and liberate Andromeda from her sea-cliff exposure and abandonment. Upon his return to Argos, while competing in some palace games, his throw of a discus went wide of it mark, striking and killing Acrisius.

In August of 1995 the creators of Dana's CHANTILLY advertisements discovered the appeal of this shower of golden rain.[1] In a dramatic illustration for the perfume we see a young woman in form and color almost a copy those painted by Titian. She is running from a dark and undifferentiated background, her deep brown hair tossing, her soft white organza skirts flowing from an embroidered and bejeweled bodice. Falling upon her are fine golden drops. Even as she flees she turns to catch some of these droplets in her hand. A single phrase accompanies the ad: "The Spray Lingerie." A spray bottle of CHANTILLY appears in the lower right corner. The illustration evokes mystery and drama.

What is its message, and why this image? To the uninformed it might seem the company sells lingerie, not perfume. Or is the model wearing beneath her gown only CHANTILLY as her lingerie? The first option is misleading, the second

[1] The advertisement first appeared in August, 1995, in *Glamour* and similar magazines.

possible but uncertain. The better suggestion is that a spray of CHANTILLY makes a woman feel like she is wearing a romantic white slip, even if she is, in truth, attired in a business suit (a trope used often in Victoria's Secret catalogs). To understand this ad the viewer must invent a situation only hinted at in the ambiguous illustration, must draw upon cultural knowledge to clarify the image. For the picture clearly has mythic echoes, it openly recalls Renaissance paintings of the Danaë story, and thus the assumption that this myth is the ad's inspiration is surely correct. We must know the whole story, however, to understand the advertisement's full meaning. We must know that Zeus' secret and ingenious entry to the enclosed princess has a happy ending, that a great hero will be born from this impregnating rain. If the viewer takes the time to ponder the suggestions offered by this advertisement's picture, she will recognize its power. A spray of CHANTILLY, a rain of golden droplets clothes a woman in romance and suggests that she may well create a hero to play a role in an heroic world.[2]

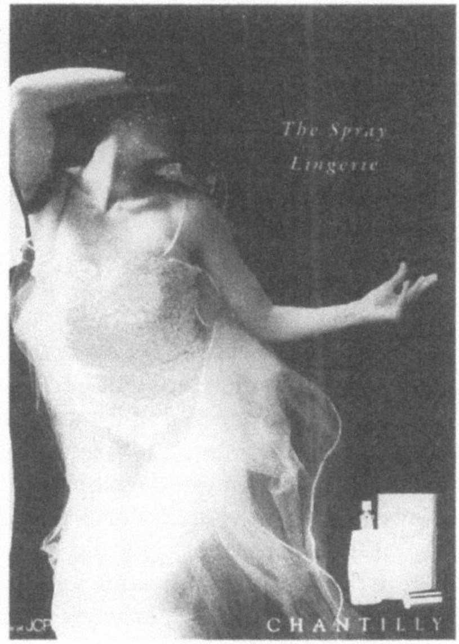

3.1 Dana: CHANTILLY

In the story of Europa and Zeus, the king of gods and men took the form of a bull. Gamboling about the pasture of the Tyrian palace, he attracted the object of his desire, the princess Europa. First she wove garlands for his horns, then climbed upon his back for a ride around the meadow. At once the bull-god turned to the sea and rushing into the waves carried Europa off to Crete. There he revealed his true

[2] CHANTILLY advertisements had a history of classical inspiration, a history which underscores the interpretation given here. In 1965 the illustration for "Nice girls do wear CHANTILLY," was the bust of a Victorian cupid resting on an embroidered pink puff. In 1970 the fragrance was advertised with the head of a woman whose hair was dressed in the style of the upper class women of Rome. The slogan for this promotion was "CHANTILLY can shake your world (and his)" but the model was seductively calm.

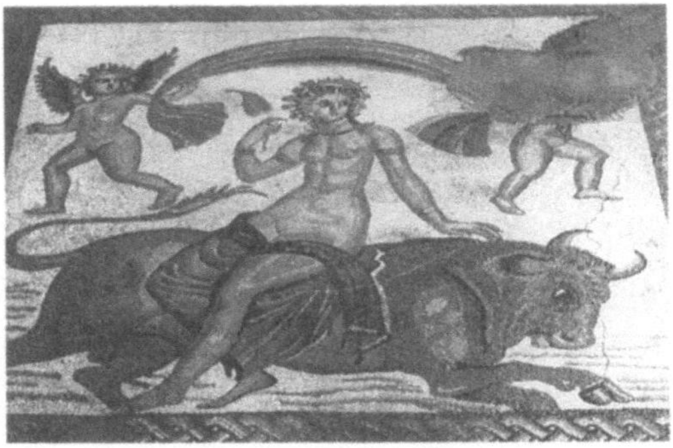

3.2 Europa & the Bull.
Mosaic.
Argos \ Archaeological
Museum

identity and from the mating of god and princess were born the legendary kings of Crete: Minos, Sarpedon and Rhadamnathus. While Europa gives her name to the continent where western civilization will develop, Minos became the eponymous leader of the civilization developing on the island. In due time another bull and a bull-man, the Minotaur, became part of Cretan myth. These myths were popular with the ancient artists, nor did the story's appeal end with the classical era: paintings and statues of Europa and the bull and of the Minotaur may be found in every museum and in the artwork from every time period. Europa and Zeus-bull and the Minotaur have also appeared in several modern advertisements.

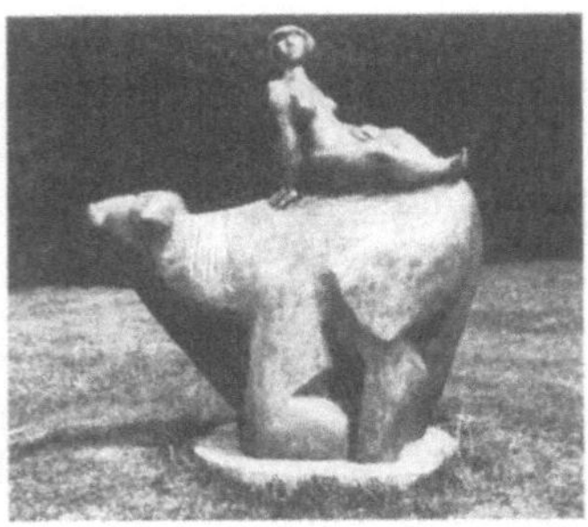

3.3 Europa. Zimmer.
Sculpture Garden \ Trier

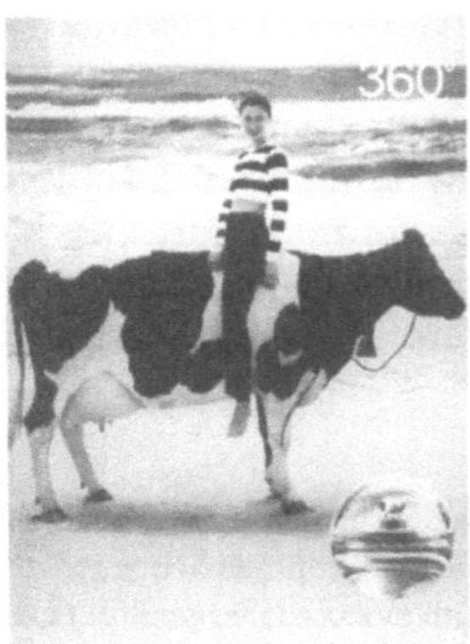

3.4 Perry Ellis: *360°*

At times the admakers play off our awareness of a classical image, play with a classical conceit. In a 1994 advertisements for its *360°* perfume, PERRY ELLIS appears to start from this familiar myth when he places a woman on a bovine creature by the sea.[3] But *360°* reverses the image: the lady faces backwards, and she is on a cow, not a bull. The ad's text reads, "Life

[3]Among numerous magazines, the advertisement appeared in *Vogue* (February, 1994).

is how you change it," giving a further indication that the illustration started with the familiar story. In this striking visual, the myth's parts are all there, but altered. The meaning, however, remains ambiguous. What is the viewer to assume? If she wears this scent, what happens? Will she be carried off to a distant isle by a god in disguise? Will the general affairs of her life turn around? Is this a good thing? This advertisement is visually arresting, while its considerable ambiguity makes it memorable.

Perhaps the boldest use of a Zeus story appeared in an advertisement taking the Leda and the Swan myth as its subject. When the king of the gods was attracted to Leda, Queen of Sparta, he disguised himself as a swan and in this avian form seduced her. In due time Leda laid two eggs, one with the divinely engendered Helen and Polydeuces; the other hatched Clytemnestra and Castor, sired by Leda's mortal husband Tyndareus. The mating of swan and woman was a favorite subject for the ancient artist: vase paintings, sculptures and steles record the erotic moment. The bizarre union appealed to the post-classical artist as well; Salvador Dali and Paul Gauguin, for instance, painted the unusual pair, although their pictures are not particularly erotic.[4]

Thus when Helmut Newton decided to focus upon this legend as part of his advertising portfolio for 1994, he had numerous examples from which to choose. The final advertisement is not, however, a direct replica of any of the existing versions, but rather a unique creation. In the June, 1994 issue of *Vogue*, photographer Newton took a series of pictures using the story of Leda and the swan to promote various high-fashion dresses. The picture astonishes while the printed text describes the visual image:

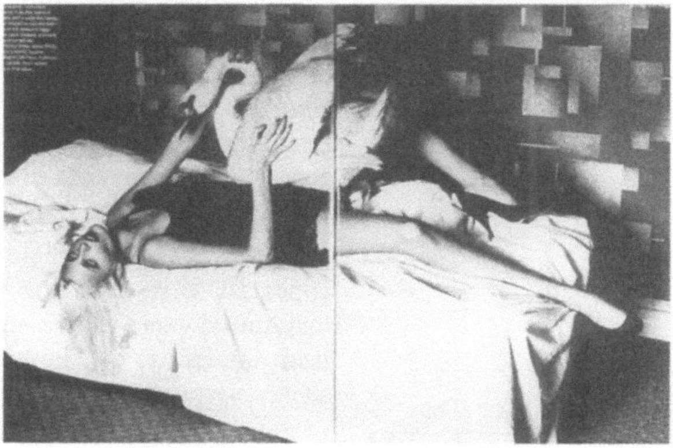

3.5 Helmut Newton for *Complice*.

[4] William Butler Yeats wrote a poem on the subject that is boldly erotic, "Leda and the Swan," published in Norman A. Jeffar, ed. *Poems of William Butler Yeats* (New York Macmillan, 1951): 247.

"Typical of Newton's sexually provocative, voyeuristic visions: A stuffed stand-in poses with a Leda-like Nadja. Also draped across the bed—one of the season's leggy little black dresses, a skimpy lace-trimmed slip. *Complice* dress, about $630." To understand this ad the viewer must know the story of Leda and Zeus/Swan. The woman about to purchase this dress must also wonder about the message the advertisement implies, for it would seem dangerous to wear this little number: will the purchase of this dress result in an avian rape or merely attract divine attention?[5] The woman who dares to purchase this dress must be one who wishes to step boldly beyond convention. Like the PERRY ELLIS *360°* advertisement, the ambiguity of this image renders it memorable, although here, with the copywriter identifying the legend, the mythologically aware shopper buys with her eyes wide open.

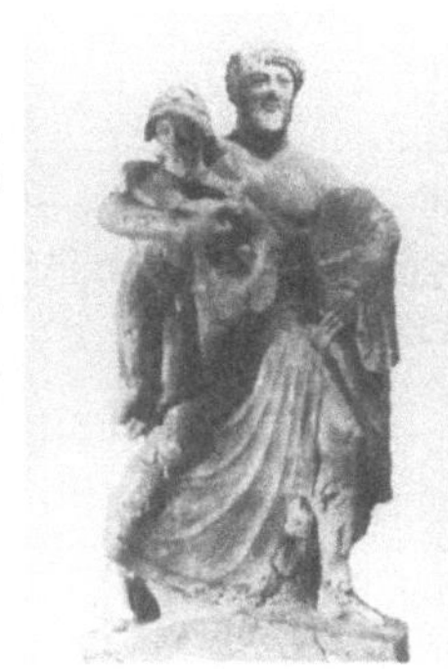

3.6 Zeus & Ganymede. Olympia \ Archaeological Museum

Zeus, like many Greek gods, was attracted to the beauty of young boys as well as that of young maidens. The best known story of such passion is that of Zeus and Ganymede. The myth has more than one interpretation. According to one version, Zeus found the Trojan prince Ganymede so beautiful that he thought his beauty would enhance the halls of Mt. Olympus and thus for his beauty alone stole him away to be cup-bearer to the gods. The other version suggests that Zeus found the youth's appearance irresistible and stole him away for erotic reasons as well as to make him cup-bearer. In the late 1980s an advertisement based on this legend appeared, this time for Cyprus Sherry. Here the inspiration came from a legend portrayed in a mosaic from the House of Theseus on Cyprus. The Cypriot sherry advertisement copied the Cypriot mosaic for its

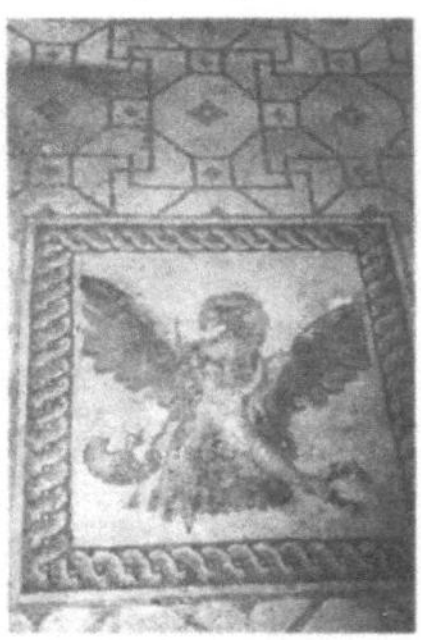

3.7 Zeus & Ganymede. Mosaic. Cyprus \ House of Theseus

[5] A demure version of this story (it seems) appeared in the August 15, 1950 issue of *Vogue*. Here Mandelbaum Coats advertised its Grand Illusion Gabardine suit on a perfectly tailored model standing before an ancient column—with a swan (statue) poised beside her. The bird is purely gratuitous to the picture, unless the myth is to be recalled, giving a subtle twist to the suit's name: Zeus as swan was indeed a "grand illusion."

visual and added words of double-entendre: "Remember a bottle when you pick up the Christmas bird." As the ad appeared on posters throughout London tube stations as well as in magazines on both sides of the Atlantic, the ad's meaning was easily understood by its audience. In this advertisement lurks no ambiguous fear, and its humor probably encouraged the purchase of the Cypriot wine.

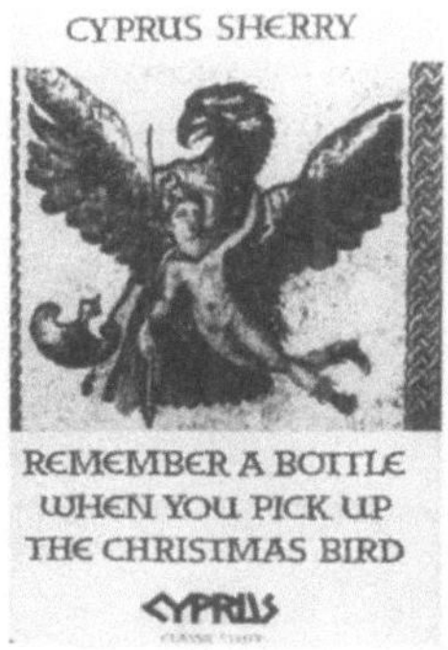

3.8. Cyprus Sherry

DIONYSUS

The amorous passion of Zeus, king of gods and men underlies the story of Semele and her son Dionysus. Zeus had become the lover of Semele, daughter of King Cadmus of Thebes, but had done so without revealing his true identity. Then Hera, jealous wife (and sister) of Zeus stepped in: she encouraged Semele, already pregnant by Zeus, to request that her lover reveal himself in his true form. The deity reluctantly granted Semele her request and the lightning which flashed around the god consumed the poor girl in its flames. But divine offspring cannot be allowed to perish; Zeus snatched from Semele's ashes the unborn child and sewed the infant into his own thigh. In due time the baby-god was born; thus did Dionysus enter the world. This divinity of double-birth held sway over the regenerative powers of nature, he symbolized the dying of the crops in the fall and their rebirth in the spring. Within Dionysus lay, it has been said, the power of "all the mysterious and uncontrollable tides that ebb and flow in the life of nature."[6] Dionysus also gave the vine and wine to mortals, a gift to soothe their pain.[7] Under the Alexandrians and the Romans in particular, Dionysus became primarily the god of wine, "jolly Bacchus" promoting an excessive indulgence in his gift to mortals. And thus it is that the god's image adorns many a wine list or menu today.

---

[6] So E.R. Dodds in his masterful introduction to his edited edition of Euripides' *Bacchae* (Oxford: 1960^2) xii:

> "He is ..the power in the tree; he is the blossom-bringer, the fruit-bringer, the abundance of life. His domain is the whole of the liquid nature, not only the liquid fire in the grape, but the sap thrusting in a young tree, the blood pounding in the veins of a young animal...."

[7] As Teiresias says in Euripides' *Bacchae* (278-283).

In antiquity, in ancient Greece, Dionysus' association with wild nature underlay his rites. Those who followed this god were frequently women, who could escape from the tedium of their looms by celebrating the Dionysiac festivals with woodland dancing. As the Athenian playwright Euripides tells the story in his play *The Bacchae*, women would go to the woods and mountain and live in peaceful association with nature— until their rites were spied upon by men. Then violence would break out, and their pinecone-tipped staffs become unerring and deadly weapons.

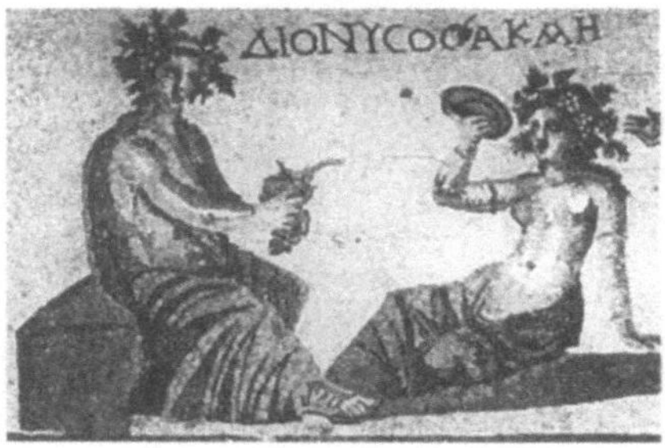

3.9 Dionysus & Maenad. Cyprus \ House of Theseus

The picture of women in unrestrained dancing was, perhaps, the most popular subject for the ancient vase painters: vase after vase portrays these bacchantes, these *maenads* (as they are often called) dancing, often in the company of Satyrs, the half-man half-goat followers of Dionysus. The unrestrained woman at one with nature has appealed to artists ever since the classical period as well, and this attraction has also spilled over into the realm of advertising.

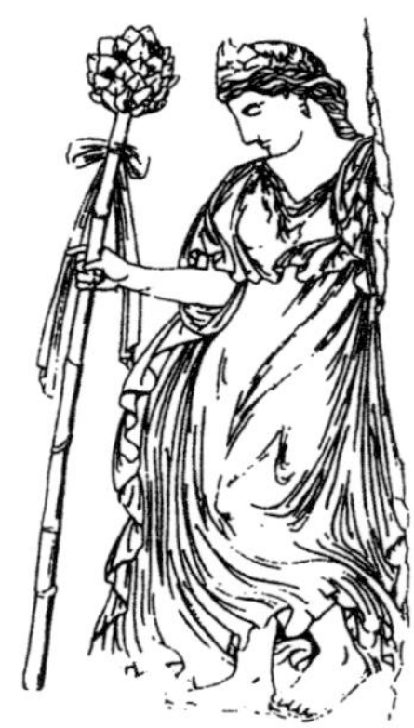

3.10 Maenad. Stele. New York \ Metropolitan Museum. Drawing by Desmond Jackson

In some advertising campaigns the Dionysiac has been carried to an extreme with men and women in exotic poses placed in strange landscapes. The best known of these are those mounted by GIANNI VERSACE. Indeed, such are the illustrations for his fashionable clothes that one might well say that his models form a *thiasos* (as the sacred band of Dionysiac followers was called) for his promotions. VERSACE advertisements suggest the abandon of the mountain-dancing maenads even when the models are immobile, while the "action" shots fully support the wild freedom offered those who follow the god of life's liquid forces.

In February of 1993, for example, Gianni VERSACE purchased 10 pages of the *New Yorker* to announce his "Collezione Primavera/ Estate 1993 (Milano)." The opening image is a bust shot of a male and female, close together, arms entwined, who seem to be emerging from the pliant object (a smooth tree trunk? a large bolster? a soft bed?) before them. His hair is long, dark and smooth, hers long and slightly mussed; a simple scarf is draped across his shoulder and chest. They stare dispassionately at their viewer.[8] Nothing about the image suggests clothing of any type: this is a lead-in picture, inviting its audience to turn the page and see what the *collezione primavera* offers. Still the illustration is striking, for the models seem to be both deadly calm while caught in violent actions. In the following pages male and female alike wear clothing from the briefest to full coverage, from most suggestive to most demure. Whether pictured alone or in a group, whether motionless or caught in actions either carefully controlled or swirling in abandon, the models suggest that these clothes take their wearer to a realm where few will feel they are in a familiar destination. Thus presented the spring collection offers surrealism and an escape from the routine of daily life. A further single-page advertisement supports the thesis that VERSACE follows the spirit of Dionysus, that his promotions suggest the abandon of the mountain-dancing maenads even when the models are immobile, while the "action" shots fully support the wild freedom offered those who follow the god of life's liquid forces.

Dionysus represents the rebirth of spring, but to be reborn he must die with the crops in the fall. In VERSACE, however, the vitality of the Dionysiac spirit continued in the fall advertisements as well. The September 1993 illustrations presented a male with wild curling hair, barely clad (if at all), supporting a woman who appears to in the grip of some type of uncontrolled emotion. Her limbs are contorted, her hair is tossing as if from a frenzied turn of her head. Her dress (which is, after all, the object to be admired!) is long, dark and clinging; it might be an appropriate attire for a sophisticated party or a night in a theater box, but does not seem well suited for the model's passionate action. Again the advertisement is visually arresting: it is hard to turn the page quickly, but will this picture draw man or woman to the nearest boutique to purchase the dress? For the most part, the casual shopper might be hard put to say what VERSACE's styles are, for very little of the clothing actually appears in the photographs. For the stylistically smart and mythologically aware, however, the illustrations attract because they create the VERSACE mood: bold, daring, in communication with one's self and with others

[8] The facial expression of VERSACE's models reflects the calm features of Cellini's Medusa, the image lying behind the VERSACE logo. In the Florentine statue, however, the Gorgon's eyes are closed, seeming to indicate the end of her power. The VERSACE models keep an arresting gaze. Cellini's interpretation, however, is not consistent with the ancient legend. According to Apollodorus (2.34ff), Perseus was able to use the head of Medusa as a weapon against the members of Polydectes' court who had abused him, while in its final resting place on the shield of Athena Medusa's head maintained its apotropaic power.

who share the oneness with nature that his clothes assert. In the VERSACE advertisements, we do not so much see particulars as generalizations about his ideas and the image he wants to promote. Gianni VERSACE does more than advertise; he makes a statement via his ads: the life style he promotes is beyond that of the rich and famous, it balances on the edge of emotional abandon. Only a few could or would follow him to the realm his images portray, but the Dionysiac imagery implies that the privileged few who do so are to be appropriately rewarded.

While any wildly dancing figure could be considered to be inspired by Dionysian cult, as maenads spent much of their time in ecstatic dance, the September 1994 advertisement for Code Bleu Jeans seems to be an authentic candidate for the identification.[9] In an advertisement for these jeans offered at Younkers-Steinbach & McRae's, we are shown a black female in a joyous and graceful leap. She is turned partially away from us; the three words making up the product's name curve beside her flank.

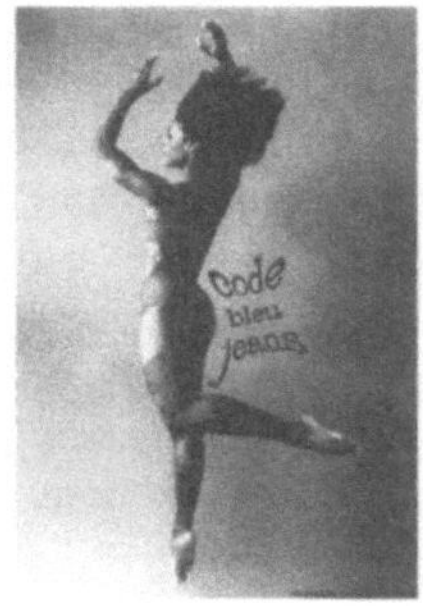

3.11 *Code Bleu*: Jeans

As with so many advertisements for apparel and jeans in particular, no example of the pants appears in the picture. The model is nude, but painted as if she were wrapped in a broad blue ribbon. "Code Bleu Jeans" is supposed to tell usall we need to know about this leisure wear. To the uninitiated, Code Bleu would seem to refer to the blue painted ribbon (if not to a hospital emergency). But to the knowledgeable reader of advertisements who comes to the magazine pages with a broad background in classical myth, it is clear that the purchase of Code Bleu Jeans will create a special feeling. The wearer will feel free, not restrained, joyous, will want to dance on the mountain. The woman who wears Code Bleu will think she is at one with nature.

The advertisement is striking, framed on the page like a work of art: it helps the magazine become a mini-museum of artful pictures. Here simplicity carries the message, a simplicity that works because we are familiar with ancient literature. The 1994 Code Bleu advertisement serves as an illustration of the final lines of the entry song (parodos) of Euripides' *Bacchae*:

[9] The advertisement appeared in *Mademoiselle* (September, 1994) and similar magazines.

Then delighting, like a colt by its grazing mother,
on swift-running feet, in leaps, goes the Bacchante!

[ll. 166-167]

More subtle interpretations of the bacchante appear in other advertisements. Chanel in particular has taken the woman-in-touch-with-nature as representative of its makeup and perfumes. As early as 1975 the model wearing Chanel *N° 19* was pictured to suggest a swirling bacchante (noted in Chapter II how the advertisement suggested it created another feeling.) At a time when a bottle with a story formed the illustrations for perfume advertisements, Chanel chose to portray its model with garments and hair flowing about her: this fragrance liberated a woman, set her spirit free. Free, but not wild, she is not in the throes of ecstacy; this woman is in calm control at the center of the storm Chanel *N° 19* has generated.

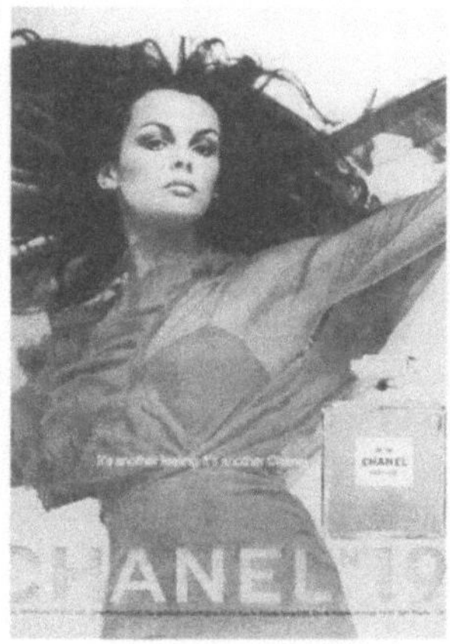

3.12 Chanel: *N°.19*

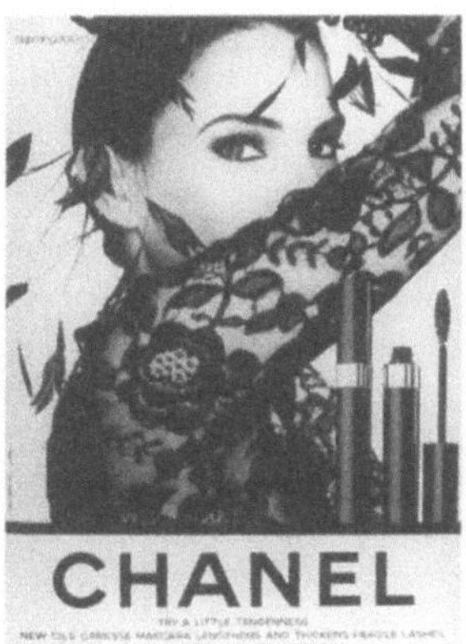

3.13 Chanel: *New Cils Caresse Mascara*

Then in the spring of 1994, Chanel came out with an advertisement for its "New Cils Caresse Mascara", with the caption "Try a little tenderness."[10] Tenderness as we think of it, however, was not what the model suggested. Shown only from the chest up, the model, dressed in a black lace blouse, bare beneath, her grey-green eyes, well-defined with black mascara looked out from behind a raised arm. Falling around her face and head were strands with leaf-shaped feathers which repeated in form the leaf and flower pattern of her black lace blouse. The entire picture evoked

[10] The advertisement appeared in many magazines, including *Glamour* (March, 1994).

the exotic, the wild, the untamed. The Chanel woman was a maenad, clad in lace and the feathers from some captured bird. She was at one with nature by being a part of it: in her leafed blouse and feather-trailing hat she appeared to united with her wild surroundings.

The mascara was touted as being especially appropriate for fragile lashes, clinically tested for sensitive eyes. This model did not look fragile (her eyes' sensitivity could not be known): her gaze showed her to be in command. Her fragility had been quenched by using the new mascara: now she was strong and bold, armed with the new power lash maker. The "tenderness" of the mascara was that of Dionysus as described by Euripides, "most terrible and most tender" (*Bacchae* 861). With Cils Caresse Mascara, a woman gained power and control. The echoes of the Dionysian gave a hint of danger to the picture, for maenads, when roused, could be very destructive indeed. It would not seem to be a good idea to cross the wearer of the new Cils Caresse Mascara from Chanel. It would be a good idea to show her respect.

From time to time the creators of an advertisement indulge in a blending of myth and art, a mixing of classical and Christian legend with post-classical art. The modern admaker is not alone in this. Early Christian iconography borrowed images of Apollo and Dionysus to promote the new cult. Apollo as good shepherd became the model for Christ with His flock, while the rays of the sun god formed the halo of the Christian deity. The understanding of Dionysus reborn made the concept of Jesus' resurrection easier to comprehend. Only when the central image of Christianity became the crucifixion did classical models fade away. The idea that a god might suffer for mortals had no place in ancient Greek belief.

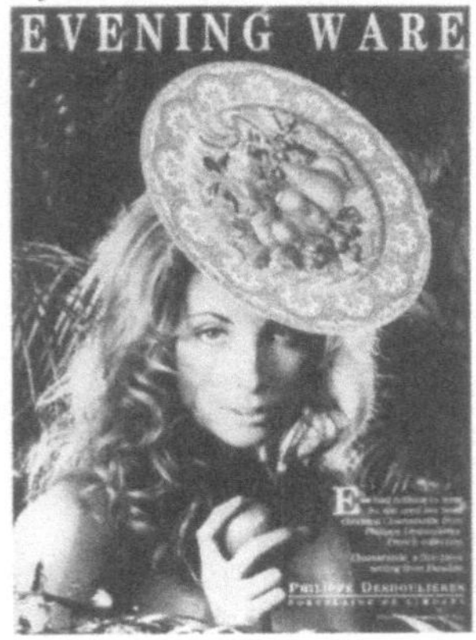

3.14 Limoges: *Chamarande*

Thus in its 1992 advertisements Porcelaine de Limoges designed an eye-catching illustration that toys with familiar images and ideas.[11] Under a title EVENING WARE we see a plate of the pattern Chamarande from the Phillippe Deshouilières' collection, a pattern designed by P. Frey. Chamarande is an elaborate design: golden lace surrounds a

[11]The advertisement appeared in *Bon Appetit* (October 1992) among other magazines.

colorful branch of pears, peaches, cherries and apples; a few raspberries fill in spaces around this magical branch. But the plate is not in a table setting. It is being used as a hat by an attractive ash-blond blue-eyed woman who holds in her hand an apple the color of her hair. She is looking directly at us with a knowing gaze. Tropical plants fill the background.

Both the design of the plate and the pose of the woman suggest a Dionysian story; the whole looks rather like the well-known Caravaggio painting of Bacchus with a crown of leaves, holding a glass of wine and looking at his audience over a table laden with an abundant bowl of fruits. The Porcelain advertisement recalls that painting, although Caravaggio's deity is rather androgynous, while the woman of the Chamarande advertisement is fully feminine. The text accompanying the illustration is a small story set out in a few witty lines:

> Eve had nothing to wear. So, she used her head, choosing
> Chamarande from Philippe Deshoulières French collection.
> Chamarande, five-piece setting from Paradise.

Biblical story blends with classical myth. The illustration is definitely Dionysian, the text is jocular Christian The advertisement is eye-catching, gaining impact from its own style and from our familiarity with classical legend and Christian heritage.

APOLLO

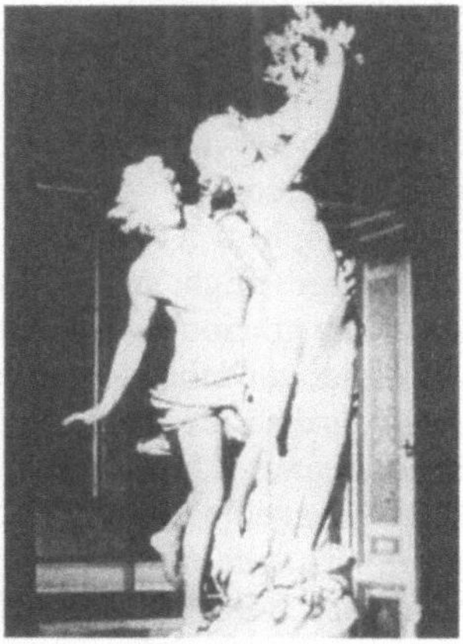

3.15 Apollo & Daphne. Bernini. Rome \ Galleria Borghese

Among the figures from the ancient pantheon appearing in modern advertising, two deities truly dominate the field, Aphrodite and Apollo. Apollo, sometimes characterized as the most Greek of Greek gods, was patron deity of many aspects of Greek life. He was originally, perhaps, a pastoral deity, looking after flocks, in charge of their health but also their disease. For like his sister divinity, Artemis, Apollo was responsible for conflicting realms of power, although the dualities within the huntress' power were more wide-ranging. Apollo was patron of the arts, especially music and poetry and thus of beauty, he guided rational thought, he revealed the future through his priestesses, the Pythia at Delphi, the Sibyl at Cumae, and at least eight other inspired women around the Mediterranean world.

Despite his patronage of rationality, the god was subject to emotion: various young girls and boys attracted his amorous attention. His loves were always tragic, however; in the end he could only watch the mortals he loved be transformed to escape his embrace or die before his eyes, and he could only offer them continued life in floral form. Thus Daphne fled his approach and became a laurel tree when her river-god father responded to her prayer for help. Apollo, embracing her bark-covered body, vowed she would be his tree, his symbol of life: the deity forever more wears a crown of laurel, victors at the Pythian games in his honor won a laurel wreath as their prize, and the burning of the bay (laurel) leaves inspired Apollo's priestess, the Pythia at Delphi, to utter her prophecies. Hyacinthus, a lad whom the god loved, was felled by an errant discus toss. As the life of the youth ebbed away, Apollo promised that he would be reborn each spring as the hyacinth. The god of rationality was left to mourn for a lost love.

While Apollo did not lay waste many to punish one, the deity did severely punish those who offended him (Marsyas) or his family (Niobe). Marsyas dared to challenge the god in a musical contest: the foolish satyr boasted that he could play the flute better than the god of music. Apollo won, and chose to flay Marsyas alive. Niobe had boasted that she was a better mother than Leto, because while the Titaness had only two children, she, Niobe, had seven sons and seven daughters. Leto's two, of course, were Apollo and Artemis, and the sibling deities banded together to slay all fourteen offspring, while Niobe herself, frozen in grief, was turned to stone, to the rocky mountain Sipylus in Asia Minor. His vengeance when not physically destructive was equally terrible: Cassandra's penalty for angering the god rendered her, I think, the most tragic of mythic figures. The Trojan princess had promised Apollo her affections, in return he gave her the gift of prophecy. She changed her mind, however, and refused his advances. He could not take back his gift, but he could change it: from then on Cassandra was doomed to know the future and to prophesy it to an unbelieving world. Even Apollo's rewards might at times be questioned, might show how little the gods of Olympus understood mortal life. To repay the gracious treatment he received when a servant at the house of Admetus, Apollo granted the king an escape from his own death upon condition that he find a willing substitute. The king of Thessaly finally learned that the god's gift was not as beneficent as it first seemed. As Euripides tells the story in his *Alcestis*, Admetus finds his aged parents are not willing substitutes, nor anyone else in his kingdom; finally his wife Alcestis agrees to die in his place. After she is gone, then and only then does Admetus realize that Apollo's gift was no reward at all.

For its JOOP! jeans Jonbil had turned to a figure of myth, Eros, in one of its most striking and unusual ads in its "Just a Thought" series (as noted in Chapter I; see further below). The company continued the classical theme and its "Just a Thought" series in its advertisements in the fall of 1995.[12] This time Apollo was the mythological figure. Filling one page of the two page spread is the head of an Apollo statue, seen in profile. Brimming from his right eye is a large green tear.

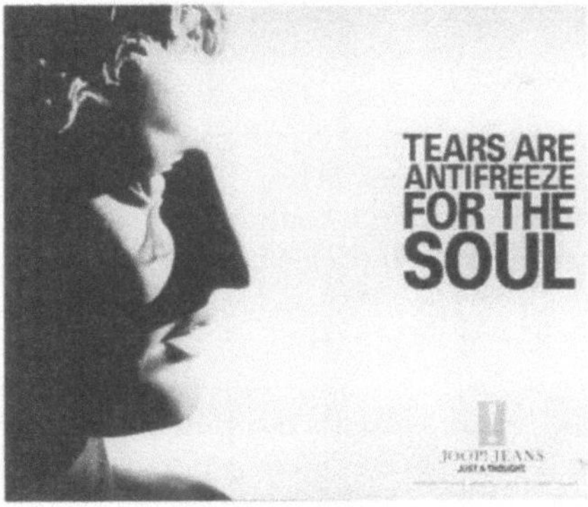

3.16 Jonbil: JOOP! Jeans

A text fills the facing page (again, no jeans appear in this advertisement): TEARS ARE ANTIFREEZE FOR THE SOUL. This "Thought" has a number of possible interpretations, but of interest to this study is the choice of image to carry the mental message. Why was a classic statue of Apollo selected? Surely anyone's tear would have had a similar implication: those who melt in tears and release their emotions free themselves from frozen sorrow. While the image does create a startling juxtaposition, a human tear replaced by a deadly automotive compound, a statue by a modern sculptor, or even a live model, would have made the same impact.

Apollo's visage is universal and immediately recognizable, perhaps the best known through art of any of the Greek male pantheon. JOOP! offers no text to explain the deity's grief; we are to know he is the god who suffered with mortals and who experienced their grief, a god who could weep for mortal pain. This gives JOOP!'s theme a powerful impact.

---

[12] The advertisement appeared in numerous magazines in the fall of 1995, including *Esquire* (September, 1995).

By choosing a deity of a pagan cult, the advertiser commits no impiety. By choosing a classic statue from antiquity to weep a tear of automotive fluid, ancient and modern are cleverly combined to make the idea timeless. The use of mythological figures for its "Just a Thought" series has given JOOP! an exciting medium for its message.

Cosmair likes to enhance its L'OREAL advertisements with classical images. In the summer of 1995 the company introduced a new coverage makeup. To promote this new "invisible coverage" the advertisement portrayed the face of a model (Heather) in front of a bust of Apollo.[13] Indeed, she seems to replace the classic head; he appears to be looking at her. The text reads, "Coverage so invisible, it's time to rewrite history!" The more complete description of the makeup begins, "It's history in the making. From L'OREAL ..." The beautiful model, "... wearing New Visuelle Invisible Coverage Make up in Beige Blush" could be pictured alone; she really needs no additional adornment.

But the classical statue adds to the image Cosmair/L'OREAL wants to promote. Her beauty is itself classical, thereby it defines beauty, sets a standard for it, for the art of the Greco-Roman world has set the pattern for modern ideas of perfection. To take the meaning somewhat further, it is her beauty that has attracted the attention of the statue: the male figure is turned to look at Heather. Even an Apollo, the most handsome of ancient deities, takes notice of the modern model. The intent it clear: the new face, enhanced with new Visuelle, will supersede, if not surpass, the classic ideal of beauty, the 5th century sculpture of a Greek divinity. The model's natural beauty, using Visuelle, "so invisible, you have not to see it to believe it" shines through, even as does the marble visage of the statue.

There are many ways to introduce a product as new, there are many ways to say it surpasses the past, many ways to say that history must be rewritten. L'OREAL chose to use one of the oldest images, that of the classic GreekApollo, to tell its message. The god's bust is assumed to be so well-known that readers of the advertisement will understand the reference: Heather's face will become the new standard for ideal beauty.

[13] The advertisement appeared in: *Seventeen* (October, 1995) among other places.

APHRODITE

The most popular deity in the advertising world by far is Aphrodite, goddess of love, goddess of sexual love, to be exact, a goddess whose power is great over both mortals and divinities. As noted above (Chapter II) the legend of her birth shows that from her very generation she is associated with both sex and the sea: Aphrodite formed in the sea foam gathered around the castrated genitals of Ouranos which his son Cronos flung into the ocean.

Cronos had attacked his father Ouranos in this way at the instigation of his mother, Gaea. The great Earth Goddess was angry with her sky husband because he rejected and tried to destroy their less-than-perfect children. In his *Theogony*, the story of the world's creation and the earliest mythological text, Hesiod tells the archetypical story (155-210). There he vividly describes how Cronos offered to help his mother against his "hateful father," how he lay in ambush with a great gray sickle and how he cut away Ouranos' members when the god of the sky approached the goddess of the earth. This is the legend that lies behind the generation of the love goddess who arose from the foam and the sea. She came ashore on the island of Cyprus—or perhaps Cythera, both islands claimed her—, wrung the water from her hair and began to direct the passions of gods and mortals.

This union of sex and surf has attracted the attention of those who create contemporary promotional copy. Sex is used to sell almost everything in recent years, and when given the opportunity to place the sexy model on the beach or in the sea itself, the ad makers have taken full advantage of the possibility. To give their illustrations more significance than mere sex, they have turned to the image of the love-goddess as the perfect model for product promotion.

Aphrodite appears in three basic styles inmodern advertising. The deity is presented as 1) rising from the sea; 2) draped with a slipping robe as the Venus di Milo; or 3) with the robe fully dropped, as the Medici Venus. When shown in the first guise, rising from the sea, we see the female eitherdirectly appearing from the waves or on a shell as Botticelli portrayed her in his "Birth of Venus". The second, goddess with slipping robe, is particularly popular. While Greek and Roman artists portrayed Aphrodite both on vases and in marble with her attire gradually slipping lower and lower over time to leave her fully revealed, today's ad artists have chosen the partially draped female as their favored image. For the sensibilities of modern America, the models are shown almost exclusively in back view,but the classical echo is clear. Perhaps because the Medici Venus' robe has fallen to the ground, this figure is never animated, but shown as the classical statue itself, whence by its presence it adds the value of an esteemed tradition to a contemporary product.

Whether a company is selling cars, handbags, perfume, or silverware, the bottom line for promotion is sex appeal, and thus the choice of Aphrodite is readily understandable. If an advertisement can suggest that by using a certain perfume, wearing a specific gown, or selecting an attractive silver pattern, a woman is nearly a goddess in her beauty, allure and understanding, she will purchase that perfume, gown, or pattern.

In the early 1990s, the love goddess was an inspiration for numerous advertisements. The most popular trope was Aphrodite Rising from the Sea. The beautiful woman rising from, or at the edge of, the sea was an image used to sell perfumes in particular, but was selected for clothing as well. Sometimes the theme was appropriate for the object being promoted, at other times the choice of woman and water seemed to have little to do with the product's name or use.

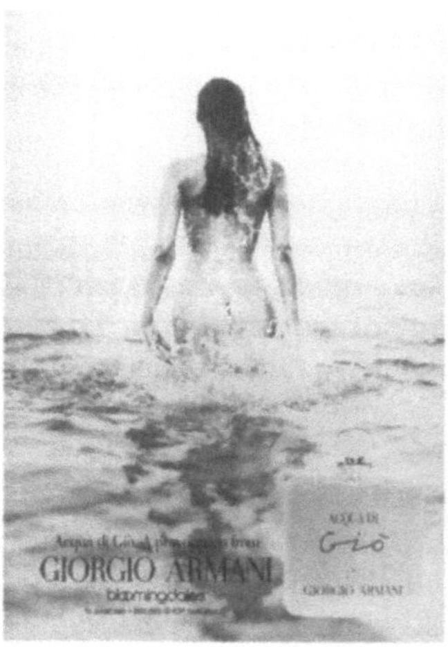

3.17 Giorgio Armani: *Acqua di Giò*

In the late summer of 1995 Giorgio Armani introduced a new perfume, *Acqua di Giò*.[14] A single sentence appears in the ad: "A provocation from Giorgio Armani." To show the appeal of the fragrance Armani chose a black and white photograph used as illustration, in which a woman, nude, walks away from the camera into the ocean; the provocation is to follow her into the sea. But this might be dangerous, and the perfume is to excite, not frighten. But because the sea foams around her and sprays across her back and hair, the model could be rising from the sea, not walking into it: she is the love goddess. Thus is the ad rendered exciting but not dangerous: we are being led to romance, not death. The sequel to this advertisement confirms the love-goddess interpretation, for in following months the perfume is advertised by the same woman, sand on her face, looking into the eyes of her viewers. In these ads Giorgio Armani played into the traditional mystique of

[14] The advertisement appeared in numerous magazines throughout the fall, among similar magazines *Glamour* (October, 1995) and *Bazaar* (October, 1995).

the sea and a woman. But his woman is not a mermaid from the realm of he fantastic; she is very much a real figure.

As usual in perfume advertisements, there is no olfactory clueas to the scent's aroma.[15] The creator of the perfume and its inaugural promotion trusted that the modern woman would know Greek myth. To the educated buyer the appeal of *Acqua di Giò* is powerful: as Sophocles said, "Aphrodite is the goddess against whom no one may stand."[16] The woman who chooses to wear this scent will conquer those whom she desires to master. Her allure comes from familiar mythology: the woman who wears*Acqua di Giò* will be as appealing as Aphrodite.

In numerous magazines during fall 1994 and spring 1995, Coty's advertisements for LONGING appeared with the slogan "Make a Man Remember." Additional text added: "Every-where he goes... Everything he sees... Everywhere he looks.. You're there." The ad's scene is a beach at the waves' break line, where a woman in a white and pink slip, possibly a nightgown, reclines as the waves break over her. The foam of the waves blends and repeats the white lace of her slip/gown. Her eyes are closed. A man in trousers and leather jacket stands at edge of scene, gazing into the distance beyond the woman. He does not seethis woman, but one of his imagination; we are to assume that the dreaming woman is the subject of his dreams.

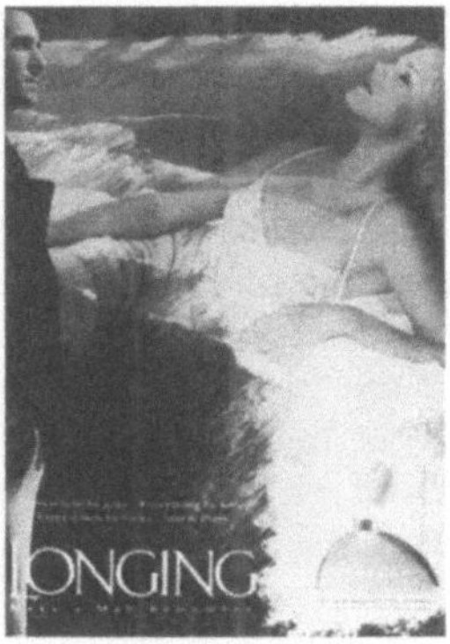

3.18 Coty: LONGING

The flower-topped bottle for LONGING is shaped to recall a breaking wave, although its shape also suggests a woman's breast. Nothing about the scene suggests the fragrance offered; while we are not to imagine the sea spray or the fresh salt air,

[15] See Tom Zelman, "Language and Perfume," *Advertising and Popular Culture. Studies in Variety and Versatility.* Edited Sammy Danna (Bowling Green, OH: 1992): 110, and Karelisa Hartigan, "The Muse on Madison Avenue," *Studies in Popular Culture* 18 (1996): 49-51.

[16] Sophocles, *Antigone* 781-190, celebrates the power of Eros, linked with that of Aphrodite at line 799: *amachos Aphrodita*, "unconquerable Aphrodite."

there is no clue as to whether LONGING has a floral, spice, or musk aroma; Coty has given us neither name nor visual association for it. Rather the ad attempts to personalize the scent: each man will remember his love when he catches a whiff of this perfume. The woman portrayed is not particularly sexy; she is attractive, yes, but compared to the women featured in some advertisements, this woman is truly demure, and surely that is intended. This is a perfume for a woman with whom a relationship will last, a woman a man will not forget, one he will remember. She is the one he will marry and long love.

Myth once again assists the eroticism the ad's creator needed to portray. He could have placed the same woman, similarly attired, in a flowery meadow, or, to be especially appealing to a man, by a cool mountain stream. But he chose the wave-break point of the sea. The reclining woman appears to be emerging from the sea itself, rising from the foam of the waves. The foam also serves to cushion the woman, supporting her weight as she rests on her arm: the foam, though appearing soft, must be firm--it acts like a shell to protect her from the inevitably rushing sand. This woman is Aphrodite, born of the sea foam, carried ashore on her half-shell, as ancient artists so frequently portrayed her. In antiquity the goddess reclined on her shell; it was Botticelli that made her stand on it. If the advertisement is understood in terms of its mythic echoes, its message can be better understood. LONGING is an erotic perfume that suggests its wearer to the man who remembers how appealing he found the woman who wears LONGING to be.

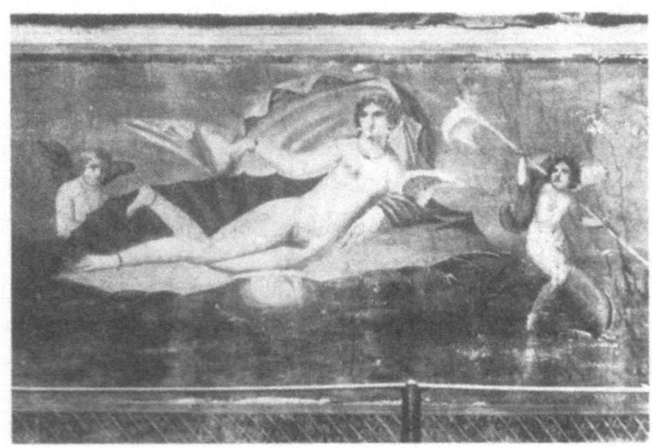

3.19 Venus Fresco. Pompeii \ House of Venus

Coty recalled Aphrodite in its promotions for VANILLA MUSK as well. The scene was consistently advertised in 1994-1995 with the back view of a naked, dark-haired woman. Her body is beautiful, appearing sculpted rather than formed of real flesh.

Her torso is turned in classic contra-posto style, so although we do not see her whole body we know what her stance would be. She is lighted so that one side is in full shadow, the other darkly visible. Her lighted side is at head, shoulder & waist labeled "NATURAL INNOCENT ROMANTIC" while on the shadowed side are the words "SENSUAL PASSIONATE MYSTERIOUS." The slogan for VANILLA MUSK is "A New Fragrance of Extraordinary Elegance."

We know what vanilla smells like, an aroma underscoring what appears to have become the flavor of the decade. In this new perfume Coty has anticipated the switch to chocolate's partner/opposite. The picture and the words suggest that the wearer of VANILLA MUSK will make an impression far more powerful than the traditional idea of vanilla. While the image is not immediately evocative of any ancient myth, its classical style draws it to our attention.[17]

With only a slight variation in the illustration, Guerlain ran the same advertisements for its perfume for many months of 1994-1995. In a tripartite series a triangular white window frames a woman; in one view she is in garden, in the other she stands at sunset beside a calm sea.

Both scenes are evocative of Aphrodite, goddess of gardens, goddess from the sea. The Guerlain woman, with her slipping robe, appears to blend into the water in which she is standing; it is difficult to see where the sea stops and the woman begins, she seems a part of the element in which she quietly stands. This might well be the moment the love-goddess steps from the water at Cythera or at Cyprus as both sites claimed her for their own. Beauty, mystery, and mythic echoes are designed to arouse both the potential wearer of the scent and the wearer's potential lover; Guerlain's ad is very effective. While we have no idea of the perfume's aroma, we do know that a woman wearing it shares a divinity's appeal.

The romance of black pearls might be variously evoked: individually, mounted in jewelry, or even at their moment of discovery. Or they could be pictured adorning a beautiful woman as she prepares for a special occasion. In 1995 Elizabeth Taylor promoted her new fragrance, BLACK PEARLS, with another illustration.[18] The pearls are mounted and do adorn a beautiful woman. But the woman is shown emerging from a nighttime sea. Under the caption "The Romance

---

[17] A very similar advertisement was designed for the new perfume *One*, only its illustration showed the model (still back view) reclining with a single drape over her. The nude or almost nude figure will be repeated frequently in various advertisements created in the next few months.

[18] The advertisement appeared, among other places, in *Glamour* (October 1995).

of Night" rises the head and shoulders of a woman clad in evening dress and wearing a long strand of black pearls.

Apart from the moonlight on the water, there is nothing particular to suggest that this is a moment illustrative of the "romance of night." The woman's cool classic beauty, her face almost like a marble statue, suggests that the romance here lies in the myth she recalls, and the message it gives: the woman who wears BLACK PEARLS will have the power of Aphrodite with her. Suddenly the Elizabeth Taylor ad resonates with suggestion: this striking beauty with her intent gaze will bring romance to the night, and her allure will be irresistible.

In a full page advertisement in the 1996 May magazines, DONNAKARAN introduced her signature bath and body perfume. The fragrance comes in a tall sleek teardrop shaped blue bottle; while striking, it is the accompanying illustration that sells the product. The model using the bath oil is portrayed with a duality of Aphrodite images. She is nude, facing away from the viewer (as is typical) and seems to rise from the circle of the bath oil's foam. She is wringing out her hair. The white froth surrounds her both as the sea and as a slipping robe. DONNAKARAN'S bath oil will render its user a goddess and a work of art, for the illustration is further reminiscent of a Degas painting. It is an irresistible promotion.[19]

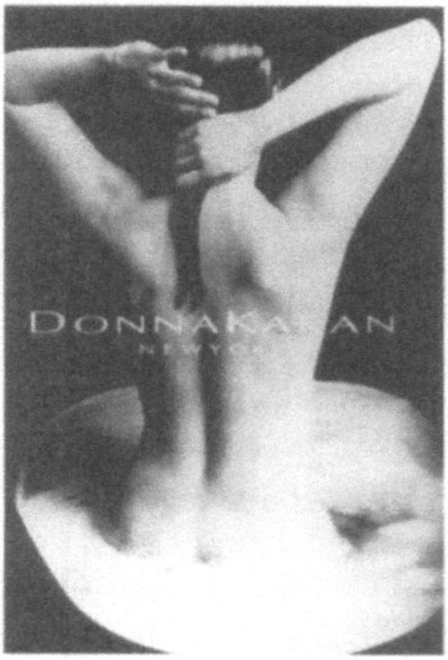

3.20 DONNAKARAN:Bath Oil

While the greater number of the Aphrodite-and-the-sea advertisements promote perfume or bath oils, from time to time the image appears for other products as well. An interesting variant on the sea-birth of the goddess was a 1996 advertisement for *iso* hair care product from the company of the same name.[20] *iso's* slogan is "change the way you

[19] A very similar image, one that certainly fell within the Aphrodite-of-the-slipping-robe paradigm, appeared on the cover of *U.S. News & World Report* of January 14, 1998, to illustrate the cover story "The Price of Vanity. Cosmetic Surgery's New Risks." The choice of picture seemed to be a direct reflection of the numerous advertisement that tempted women to become mortal love-goddesses, this time not by the use of perfume or bath oil but under a surgeon's knife.

[20] The advertisement appeared, among other places, in *Mademoiselle* (October, 1996). In the March, 1996 promotions, *iso* pictured a similarly posed woman, this time wrapped in blue, this time her golden brown hair floats out behind her as she appears to sink across the page. The

feel," but the ad's lead-in phrase was "hair reborn." The model photographed for the shampoo did not have the flowing tresses usually shown in such ads. Rather she was folded upon herself in a stylized fetal position, while a swathe of red gauze swept over her like a wave; she was floating on the black page with a mirror image appearing at the top edge of the page. Her short red hair caught the light's glow as did her skin. The allusion was to birth, rebirth by the lead phrase. Here the birth is celebrated by the allusion to that of Aphrodite from the waves of the sea.

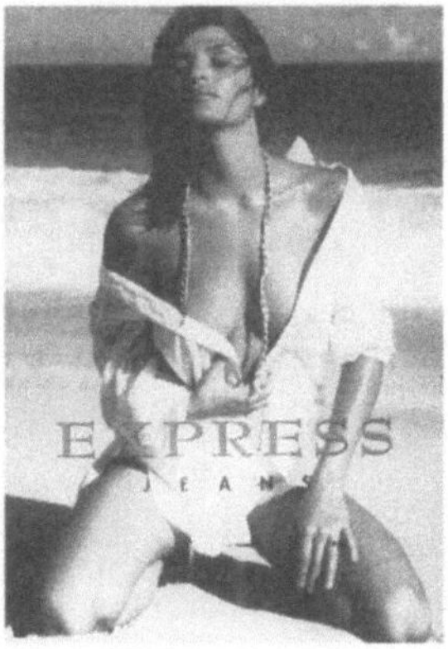

3.221 EXPRESS: Jeans

The love goddess can emerge from the sea to promote products other than those associated with a woman's toilette; she can assist the sales of clothing as well. In 1994 EXPRESS jeans placed its model on the beach. The woman kneels at the wave's break, its spray splashing over her.[21] Her blouse is open to the waist, no jeans are visible. She is very much a part of her element, a very attractive woman; anyone attired in EXPRESS jeans can share her joy and her power. The full sexuality of the picture can be appreciated without classical understanding, but if we read the image in terms both of the tradition of the ancient deity and of a modern love-goddess, the advertisement is richer, deeper, less ephemeral. Advertisements are by their very nature evocative of the present moment, but each time an ad is created at the same time is born the hope that it will remain in memory, included among those recognized all-time greats of advertising history.

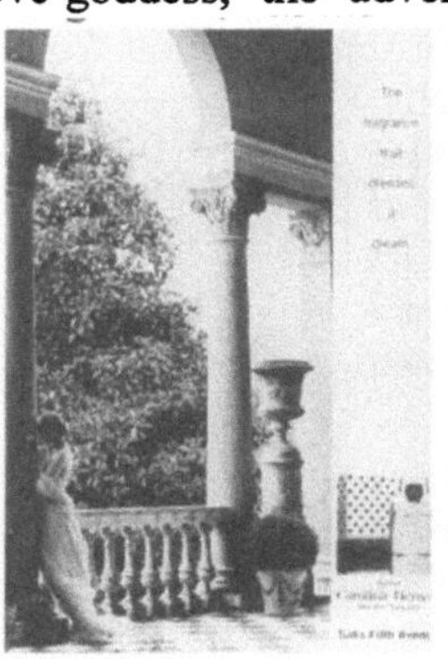

3.22 Carolina Herrera: Perfume

The Aphrodite and the slipping robe trope has been consistently most popular. It, too, is often used for perfumes, but

same double/mirror image idea is used in the March ad as well (in *Mademoiselle*, among other places).

[21] The advertisement appeared in *Vogue* (April, 1994) and most similar magazines.

other products are also promoted with this image. The woman half-clad appears in many settings, but the echo of the myth is always present.

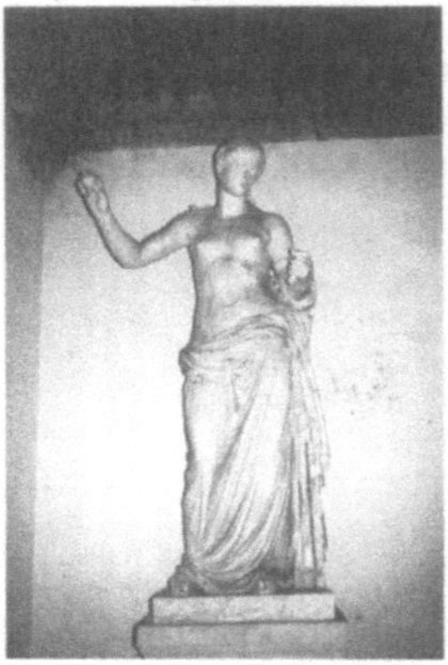

3.23 Aphrodite. Arles \ Hotel de Ville

Carolina Herrera Perfume prefers the classic style for its advertisements. With the motto "The fragrance that dresses a dream," the scent is illustrated as if that dream arose from the world of high society and an elegance expressed in Greco-Roman style. In 1994 the advertisements portrayed a young woman leaning dreamily against a Corinthian column on a marble-tiled vaulted veranda. Two large Grecian urns dominated the setting; one on a short column base, the other filled with an abundant plant, a Southern magnolia tree filled the space beyond the open arch. The setting was the old South and its neo-classical architecture.

The young woman was draped in flowing fabric slipping from her shoulders: she was immediately recognizable as an animate imitation of thefamiliar statues of Aphrodite, so frequently portrayed with a slipping robe.The model's hair is also done in classic style. Thus in appearance, attire,and setting she evokes the realm of classical myth. The dream aroused by Carolina Herrera comes from the deepest recesses of the common heritage of western society. By so illustrating this scent, the creators of this perfume play off our knowledge and perception of ancient glory and at the same time give the product an impressive pedigree. The woman who wears Carolina Herrera is both the subject of her own dream and the object of others' fantasy.

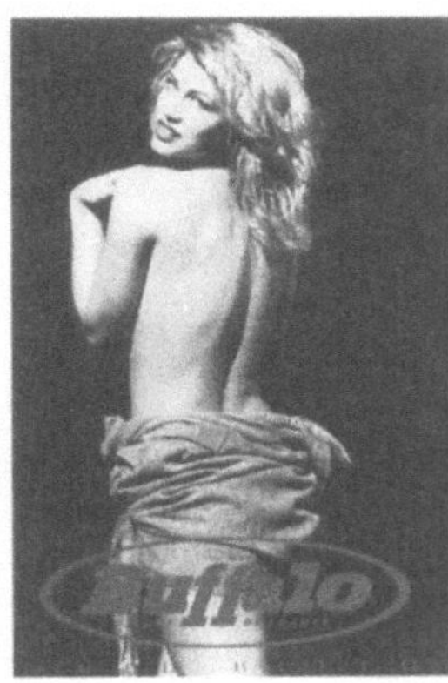

3.24 David Bitton: *Buffalo Jeans*

As it is not only perfume advertisements that use the goddess from the sea image, so the slipping robe portrayal is not limited to fragrance advertisements. The admakers for women's clothing have long realized the appeal of the love-goddess in modern dress. One of the most evocative was that created in 1994 for David Bitton's *Buffalo Jeans de*

France.[22] The blond model looks at us over her shoulder, nude but for aman's denim shirt tied casually around her buttocks. No jeans appear in the picture; as we have seen, they are seldom shown in 1990s jeans advertisements.

The woman in the slipping robe trope is so popular, indeed, that it is often used even when the product advertised has little to do with sex, a woman, or even a robe. Hence in 1995 KARASTAN offered this rather bizarre advertisement for its carpets.[23] The company often played off its slogan "You'll love the way it wears." Here the ad men have carried the slogan to its logical- or illogical-conclusion, showing a woman wearing a multicolor panel Kirman as a skirt. The advertisement taps into at least two allusions from the ancient world. The part of the carpet draped about her body looks like a wide A-line skirt: to the educated viewer, style, color and figure are reminiscent of a Minoan fresco, the dancer from Knossos, for example, or the "priestess" from Mycenaean citadel at Tiryns. The remainder of the carpet is so arranged as to suggest the woman has risen from its depth, is emerging from it as Aphrodite rose from the sea, an illusion heightened by her coiffure and classic profile. As the advertisement also blends the two tropes for the portrayal of Aphrodite it becomes a most effective illustration.

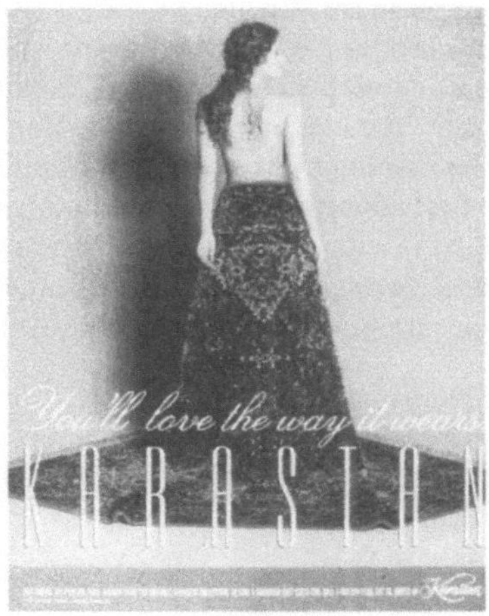

3.25 Karastan: Carpet

A person purchasing a KARASTAN does not desire to wear the rug as a garment but wants the carpet to wear well on the floor. A picture of a well-carpeted room, however, is too familiar, too common. But when the advertising agency chose to put a new spin on its slogan, offering an illustration designed to highlight the play on words, it made the viewer think of KARASTAN's carpets in a different way. Familiar myth and a new take on it made the Aphrodite-based advertisement both visually attractive and intellectually appealing.

---

[22] Among other places, the advertisement appeared in *Vogue* (September, 1994).

[23] The advertisement appeared, e.g. on the back cover of *Bon Appetit* (March, 1995).

Aphrodite's most unexpected appearance, however, was in an advertisement for bathroom fixtures. KOHLER has long taken a bold artistic approach in its advertising, with many of its advertisements featuring "works of art" created immediately for the company, identified as a number in the "As I See It" series. From time to time these "works of art" have used mythological themes for powerful artistic messages.

In the spring of 1994 KOHLER turned to classical art and legend to announce a new line of bathroom fixtures. For the illustration Dominique Isserman drew her inspiration for "the Bold Look of KOHLER" from the realm of the Greek divinities. Her black and white photography portrayed two images of goddesses, one painted, one illustrated by a live model. In the background of #11 in the "As I See It" series, we see "the elegant lines of the San Raphael□Water-Guard toilet," and #13 in the series displays "the grace of the San Raphael□ Lite□ 1-1½ Gallon toilet." The text of the first advertisement immediately defines its source by denying it: "What's sleek and trim with classic curves? The woman? Forget it." It is KOHLER'S new toilet that has classic curves. For #13, the text writer assumes we know the source, and opens simply with "an awakening.".[24]

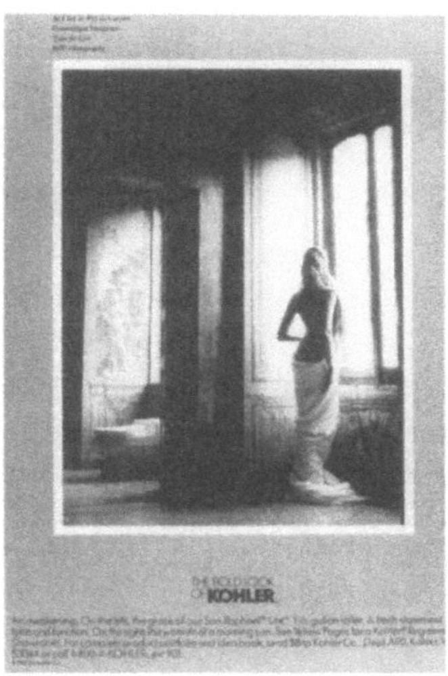

3.26 KOHLER:
San Raphael-Lite Toilet

The illustration for these advertisements shows an Artemis statue painted on the wall beside the toilet. The goddess is portrayed on a pedestal with a familiar Arcadian landscape behind her. In the foreground the mythic statement is continued. Here the classic statue of Aphrodite has been animated: a living model stands before a sunlit window. Her robe is slipping in the manner portrayed in Greek sculpture, her hair is flowing; we see her back, with the drapery falling into classic folds that seem to be carved from marble. In #13, a single enigmatic sentence describes the scene: "On the right, the warmth of a morning sun." The tall-ceiling paneled room appears as a section of an intimate museum: KOHLER fixtures are works of art.

[24] The advertisements appeared in numerous magazines, including *The New Yorker* (May 23, 1994) and *Bon Appetit* (May, 1994).

Despite the graceful lines of the toilets, however, there is nothing about them that will immediately define them as works of classic art. But enhanced with a painting on a classical theme and an animate image of Aphrodite, the message of the advertisement is evident. The placement of the figures is consistent with the works of art advertisements the company has selected as its promotional method. First the beautiful Aphrodite "statue" catches our attention; we take a double glance as we realize the familiar image is a real woman. Then our eye travels within the perspective of the picture to the toilet, and thence on to the painting of Artemis: the two "works of art" share visual and hence mental identification. KOHLER has skillfully used its audience's knowledge of myth and familiarity with classical art to promote a very basic and simple plumbing fixture. Isserman's art work has given stature to a new item by associating it with the old. The advertisement successfully elevates the ordinary to the extraordinary via its use of ancient Greek mythology.

As Apollo and Zeus found mortal women attractive, Aphrodite found several mortal men alluring. Her alliance with the Trojan prince Anchises led to the birth of Aeneas, founder of Rome. But not all her affairs had a happy outcome, and the most famous of her tragic loves was the beautiful hero Adonis. The young man came into being from a cursed and incestuous union between Myrrha and her father and when the unhappy girl was transformed into a myrrh tree, Adonis emerged from its trunk. As a baby he was tended by Aphrodite; when he grew to manhood the love-goddess found the young hunter irresistible. He preferred to pursue wild animals, risking danger despite Aphrodite's warnings. Many a Renaissance painting portrays the handsome youth leaving the pleading goddess; Shakespeare had earlier told the story as well. In time Adonis met his match in a boar and lay dying in the wood. When Aphrodite found him, all she could do was lament—and promise that from his blood a flower would spring each spring. Thus did the anemone, the first delicate bloom of the year, come into being.

Painters and sculptors have recorded Aphrodite's grief and the youth's demise as well. Whether asleep in fatigue from his hunting or relaxed in the final sleep of death, the "sleeping Adonis" became a popular subject in post-classical art. Equally well-known is a Hellenistic sculpture known as the "Sleeping Faun." Late and post-classical art inspired by myth inspired several modern advertisements. The best ads playing to this trope appeared in 1993-94 when Davidoff promoted its colognes for men, *Zino*, "fragrance of desire" and *Cool Water* by portraying a handsome man, a modern Adonis, asleep on a beach in a pose the recalls the Sleeping Faun.[25]

[25] The advertisement appeared in all popular magazines, both for men and for women, e.g.,

Whether arising from her own creation stories or from myths associated with those she loved, the advertisements inspired by Aphrodite favor a seaside setting. Love, desire, surf and sea are as closely united in the world of modern advertising as they were in the myths and stories of classical culture.

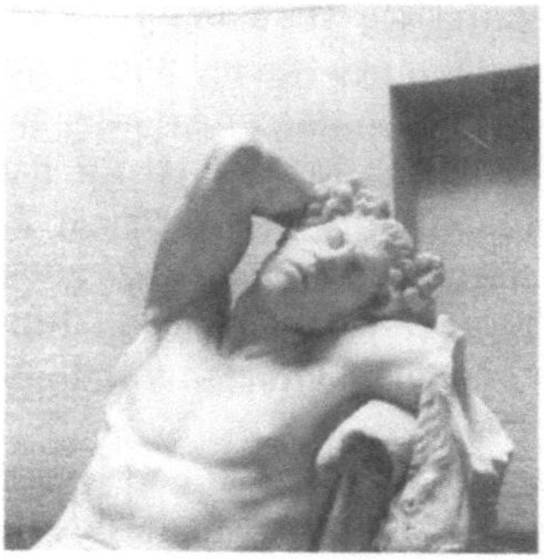

Left:
3.27
Sleeping
Fawn. Berlin
\ Glyptotech

Right:
3.28
Davidoff:
Cool Water

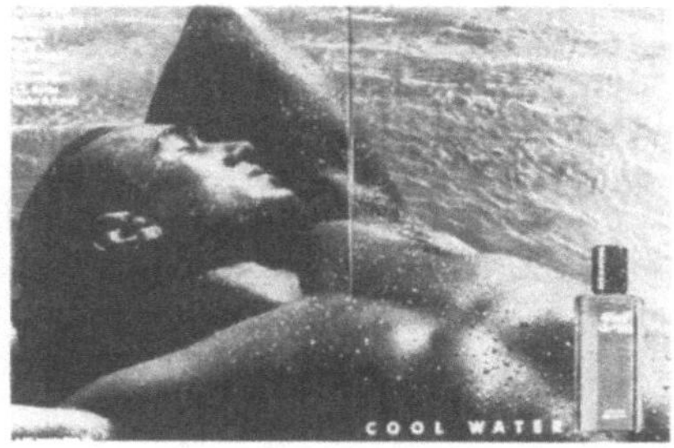

Eros, son of Aphrodite, enters the advertising world in his Hellenistic guise, i.e., as a small winged child, the Cupid of modern Valentines. Armed with his bow and arrow and fitted with wings, he adorns numerous ads to show the product's charm and, if at all possible, its erotic appeal. In ancient Greek myth, Eros was always winged, even before he was imagined as a definite anthropomorphic deity. It was the generative power of the winged god of love that brought the earlyelements of the universe together, according to Hesiod, the first to write his ideas, the first to pen a creation story. As time went on, Eros became a handsome youth, representative of the homosexual alliances of the Greek male. Even so portrayed, however, Eros had wings. The love god could fly to someone, he could also flit away; it was difficult to hold him fast.

When belief in the ancient divinities began to wane and the stories about them were more the stuff of literature than of faith, Eros was always pictured as the impish winged child, now flying about and shooting his arrows of passion at mortal men and women. He still represented the power of love, the emotion the ancients described as weakening the knees and clouding the mind. And the passion aroused by Eros, even pictured as a cheerful Cupid, remains a potent aspect of contemporary

---

Esquire (June, 1993) and *Esquire Gentleman* (Fall, 1994) and *Mademoiselle* (March, 1994).

life. If advertisements are reflections of society, Eros and Aphrodite personify the guiding principle of modern society.

A review of the many products promoted by a cheerful cherub would be long and redundant. Every once in awhile, however, Eros appears in an unusual illustration that arrests the viewer's attention. One of the best was an advertisement for JOOP! jeans. As previously noted, the Jonbil Company ran a series of advertisements entitled "Just A Thought, and in the early 1990s turned to myth for its thought. Again no jeans appear in the illustration designed to promote them.[26] At the bottom of the full page ad Eros lies supine, impaled by his own arrow. Above the pierced love god runs the text (in caps): WE HAVE DEGREES FOR MURDER BUT NOT FOR LOVE. JUST A THOUGHT! The illustration and the thought are arresting; we have no idea, of course, what the jeans are like, but such an advertisement will move the shopper to ask for them at the mall.

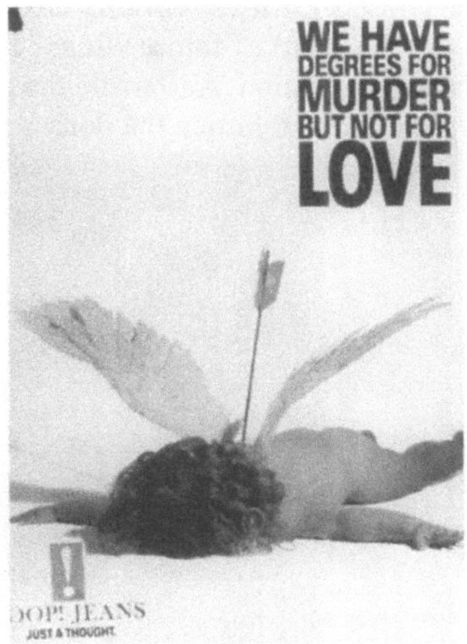

3.29 Jonbil: JOOP! Jeans

An interesting advertisement appearing in print media in the fall of 1995 was that for Geoffrey Beene's fragrance *Grey Flannel*.[27] Here an attractive man, nattily attired in his grey flannel suit (here image stands in for scent), has purchased an apple and a mango from a fruit seller; the pineapple, bananas and umbrella suggest a tropical setting for the scene. What arrests the viewer's attention, however, it not the man wearing grey flannel (suit or scent) but a small naked boy standing immediately in front of him, apparently unnoticed by him or the fruit seller. The child is about to bite into his own deep red apple. What is this unclothed tot doing in this picture?[28]

---

[26] The Eros advertisements appeared in many magazines targeted for an upscale audience; *Elle* (November, 1993) was one of these.

[27] The advertisement appeared in *Vogue* (October, 1995) and similar magazines.

[28] We cannot assume that he has just wandered into the set like the "mysterious man in

The child is almost certainly Eros. From the Hellenistic period onwards, if not earlier, this deity has been portrayed as a young child, the willful son of Aphrodite who both at her direction and on his own shoots arrows of desire into those chosen for love. On this naked child the shoulder blades are emphasized--perhaps the roots of future wings? Finally, the apple as the traditional fruit of love seals the suggestion. And while the grey flannel man does not see the love god, this is typical; he will notice the deity's power later.

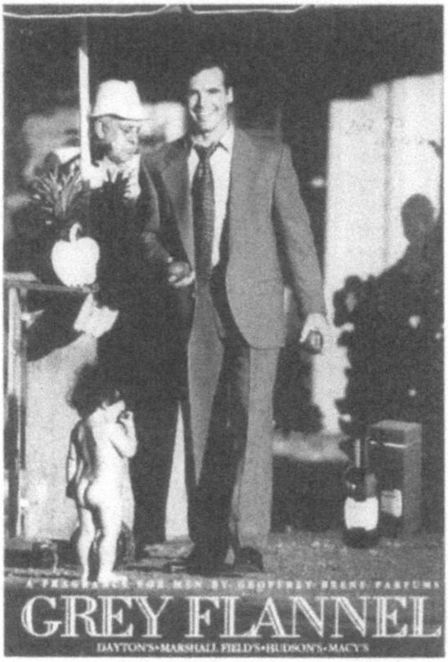

3.30 Geoffrey Beene: *Grey Flannel*

The three figures, the man, the fruit seller and the child are shown in striking clarity. This clarity of the picture serves, surprisingly, to remove it from reality: there is a sense of mystery about the scene with its deep shadows and uncertain background. Each figure seems unaware of the other, yet we know they are intimately connected: the man who bought his fruit from the impassive vendor will soon experience the power of the unnoticed child at his feet.

The wearer of Geoffrey Beene's *Grey Flannel* will find his life touched by mystery and enhanced by romance. An innocent deed-the purchase of fruit (albeit a rather exotic mango) will have exciting results. This well designed advertisement attracts attention by its striking imagery and gains impact by its subtle allusion to classical mythology.

These four deities and the legends connected to them were the inspiration for numerous classical works of art and post-classical paintings and sculptures. They played the greater role in the print - media advertisements of the early 1990s as well. But they are not the only figures from Greek and Roman myth appearing on the pages of today's magazines (nor has the appearance of the love-goddess been exhausted here). The next chapter traces the pervasive use of other ancient deities in modern advertising.

---

pajamas" that appeared in the Benson & Hedges advertisements in the late 1980s. Naked children do not just wander around shooting sites!

IV
A RICHER LIFE THROUGH CLASSICAL MYTH: ANCIENT LEGENDS ENHANCE MODERN ADVERTISING AND MODERN LIFE.

The four figures of the Greek pantheon, Zeus, Dionysus, Apollo, and Aphrodite, whose names have so often promoted women's clothing and perfume, are not the only classical deities to appear in print media advertisements for these items. Divinities of ancient myth permeate Madison Avenue's attempt to persuade the female shopper to increase her wardrobe and enhance her visual and scented appeal. While the male is encouraged to participate in enhancing his lady or his relationship with her, advertising via myth is aimed primarily at women, the articles the ancient deities promote are largely for women. But the pervasive use of classical mythology in modern ads does not by-pass the man of the house; the illustrations for a wide range of products- cars, wine and liquor, men's clothing, and household appliances (purchased by both genders)- are brought to attention via ancient legend. As Andrew Wernick points out, advertising has long combined "elements of archaic myth with a newer worship of the labouring subject...classically embodied in updated versions of Prometheus and Adam."[1] Classical art and architecture also play a role in enhancing modern products. In some promotions, a Greek or Roman statue or building is used for a simple and direct message: the item is a classic- and hence valuable. In other advertising campaigns for which the inspiration comes from the ancient world, however, the approach is more subtle, and the success of the ad rests upon the knowledge of the viewer: to understand the advertisement's message, the public must be familiar with the themes and images which have shaped western culture.

PERFUMES
Fragrances for Women

Fragrance cannot be portrayed visually. All perfume ads must rely on an evocation of mood and/or image to communicate the aroma, and thus mythological echoes are especially prevalent in the realm of perfume advertisements.[2] In a thought-provoking article titled "Language and Perfume," Tom Zelman writes:

---

[1] Andrew Wernick, *Promotional Culture. Advertising, ideology and symbolic expression.* (London and Newbury Park, CA: Sage Publications, 1991): 53-54.

[2] The "lift here to experience" strips that began to appear in magazines in the early 1990s

> There is virtually no language, either colloquial or technical, capable of describing what we smell when we consider the scent separately from its source... The vast majority of perfume advertisements make no effort to describe the scents they are promoting.[3]

Zelman is interested in the linguistic aspect of perfume ads, where as I am concerned with the images the ad makers choose, and what reactions these pictorial representations of an olfactory experience are expected to arouse.

Fragrances must first attract by name, then by aroma, so many are given names explicitly from the realm of sex, but many others are titled by mythological characters or places. Thus to be sexually alluring some perfumes, for example, are called *Obsession, Desire,* even *Tabu*, and the intent of the name is obvious. Those using a mythic name as a conceit include *Narcisse, Sirène,* or *Elysium*, and here the implication is more subtle. The user must understand that through the perfume called *Narcisse* she can admit to self-adoration; by wearing *Sirène*, she acknowledges the allure of dangerous sexual attraction;[4] or by dabbing on *Elysium* a woman can experience "Heaven on Earth."[5] Even a name not directly linked to myth, however, can be advertised with its images; as we have seen, Dana has for years promoted its very popular *Tabu* within the frame of the Pygmalion story.

Thus the admen of Madison Avenue must become mythmakers as they create the promotions for women's fragrances. For the visual elements accompanying perfume advertisements are what draw the eye to the scent and these gain power

---

show the perfume makers realized this problem. However, for the most part, readers resented the aromatic magazines that arrived in their mailboxes and so in recent years this practice has been deliberately cut back.

[3] Tom Zelman, "Language and Perfume," in *Advertising and Popular Culture. Studies in Variety and Versatility.* Ed. Sammy Danna (Bowling Green, Bowling Green UP, OH: 1992): 110.

[4] Readers of Homer's *Odyssey* might hesitate to buy this scent (see *Od* X.154-200.) In the ancient world Sirens were bird-women, whose song reporting all the world's events lured men to ruin: those who sailed by the rocks where the bird women sang were tempted to stop and listen forever to this early musical world-wide news service (a sort of proto-CNN). It is later ages that confused the overwhelming desire to know with the overpowering desires of sex.

[5] This phrase is printed with every advertisement for this perfume by Clarins; it describes the common understanding of the realm, a modernization of the Isles of the Blest (see below).

when cloaked in the mythic veil. The mythic allusion is most often conveyed in a single one-time illustration, perhaps repeated with variations in subsequent campaigns. Other companies opt to create mini-myths for their scents, carrying the story over several months, allowing it to unfold in a series of images as stories used to be serialized in newspapers and magazines for a reading public.

The advertising campaign for *Narcisse* was a promotional program that relied upon the shopper's knowledge of classical myth, presenting a study interesting for its mythological associations. The concept of narcissism is well known, but the story behind the term is perhaps less familiar.[6] Narcissus was a handsome youth, indeed, to himself, a beautiful young man, who found no one to his liking. He was seen by the nymph Echo, herself already punished by Juno for her garrulous tongue so that she could never initiate a conversation. Consumed with passion for Narcissus, she could not address him; she could only wait to repeat his own words. When Echo was finally able to approach the boy, he fled, violently refusing her advances. Spurned, she wasted away until only her voice remained. Meanwhile, another rejected lover prayed to the gods above that Narcissus might fall in love and be unable to possess his beloved. His prayer was heard. For when the youth caught sight of his own reflection in a woodland pool, he was captivated by the face he saw in its waters. But each time he reached for the image it slipped from his grasp. Echo, hearing his vain cries, repeated his "Alas!" So Narcissus remained, forgetting to eat or drink, until he finally wasted away in love for his own image. But when the nymphs went to prepare his body for burial, they found only a white flower whose petals encircled a yellow center. From his body his namesake flower had been born.

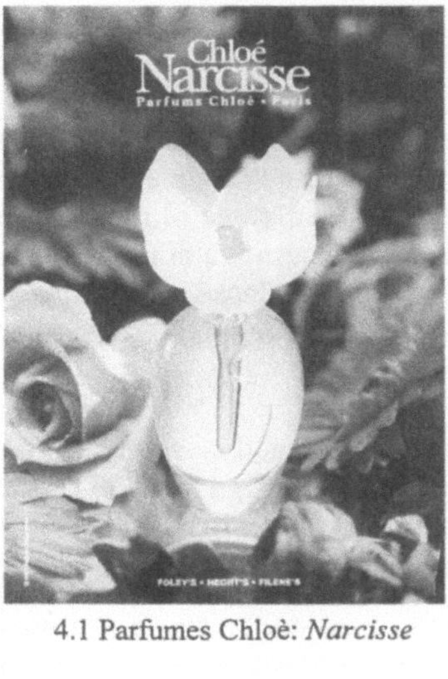

4.1 Parfumes Chloè: *Narcisse*

In the first illustration chosen to promote its new perfume *Narcisse*, PARFUMES CHLOÈ chose to let bottle stood alone, the pure white flower on it serving to attract attention; the potential buyer would look for the blossom among the perfume vials on

[6] The story is best told by Ovid in his *Metamorphoses* (3.342-510).

the perfume for the self-indulgent, the closet member of the recent me-generation; it intimates self-worship on the part of the wearer.

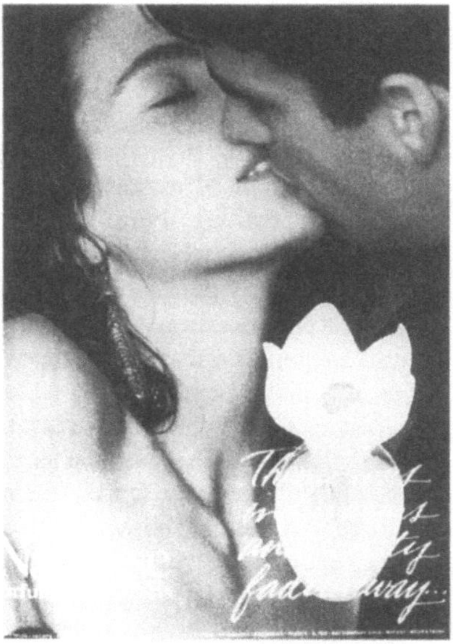

4.2 Parfumes Chloè: *Narcisse*

Thus PARFUMES CHLOÈ's advertisements for *Narcisse* began with the simple flower, leaving the buyer to understand it merely as the lovely harbinger of spring, and only the mythologically alert to realize any further implications. In the next ads, however, the self-reflexive ideas began to emerge.[7] The single flower was followed with a photograph of a woman saying, to the viewer or to herself, "All I really wanted to say was 'Kiss me.'" The next image expanded on the theme: "All I wanted was to be taken into his arms." The "kiss me" and "taken into his arms" lines were followed in close succession- indeed almost simultaneously- by a picture of the same woman, but this time her words are "Then I was in his arms and reality faded away." Wearing *Narcisse*, she had attained her desire. The final image of this sequence was a scene of rapturous and wordless embrace: the absence of words rendered the narrative of the advertising campaign itself a ring-composition. Even when the picture lacks a text, however, the woman seems inwardly focused; those knowing the legend of Narcissus can fully appreciate the intentions of the scent's creators.

What, exactly, is the scent of white linen? Estée Lauder's spring 1995 advertising campaign for WHITE LINEN offered a subtle echo of a classical theme. A bare-foot woman in a white (linen) slacks suit, with a white (unbleached muslin)

[7] The series of advertisements appeared in numerous magazines during 1994-1995, including examples in *Elle* (July 1994): the Flower; *Vogue* (October, 1992): "Kiss me"; *Cosmopolitan* (October, 1992): "Take in Arms" and *Gourmet* (March, 1993): "Reality Faded." The speechless rapture appeared, among other places, in *Cosmopolitan* (November, 1993).

shawl/scarf hurries away from the viewer on the sand dunes of a beach at sunset.[8] What are we to imagine from this sunset beach scene? Calm beauty, for it is at first glance a pretty scene, with the rays from a low sun highlighting the woman's costume. But the woman's swift gait and suggestive scarf, coupled with the seascape, undercut the positive image.

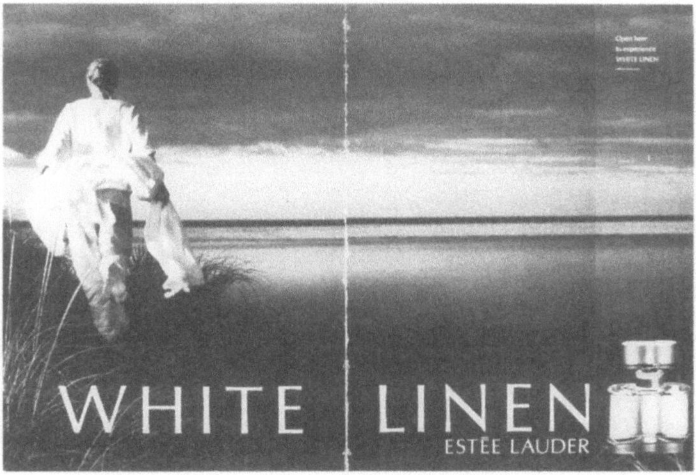

4.3 Estée Lauder: *White Linen*

There is a sense of mystery pervading the peaceful scene: the woman is alone as darkness gathers, no welcoming destination is in sight. She seems to be moving quickly- perhaps even running. Suddenly we recall tales from ancient myth: Eurydice, beloved of Orpheus, fleeing Aristaeus along the riverbank, unmindful of the deadly snake lying in the grass, Persephone in the meadow, picking flowers as Hades creeps upon her, Asteria, dashing along the coast away from Zeus, about to jump into the sea and destined to become an island, or Britomaris, who leaped into the Cretan Sea to escape her pursuer Minos and was transformed into Diktynna, net goddess of fishermen. The scarf billowing behind WHITE LINEN's model is also evocative of ancient art, for the arch of the scarf is typical of erotic scenes on vases and in the plastic arts.

The scent as portrayed evokes beauty and mystery, with a hint of danger. Suddenly WHITE LINEN becomes an erotic and dangerous perfume: it is not an aroma for the tea party or the board room. While the scene itself suggests only

[8] The advertisement appeared in many magazines, including *ELLE* (February, 1995).

aroma for the tea party or the board room. While the scene itself suggests only mystery and not dangerous love, the mythic echo the advertisement recalls offers the more complex message.

The danger lurking below the surface in this advertisement was evident to Mary Tannen, writing in the New York *Times* "Fashions of the Times" in Fall, 1998.[9] Tannen creates a biography for Estée Lauder's WHITE LINEN, tracing the advertisements for the scent from their portrayal of innocence in 1979, to the picture of a woman of brittle assurance ten years later, while women outside the advertisements were struggling with the issues of real life. Of the 1994 illustration Tannen writes, "Suddenly in 1994, you were running. Fleeing your garden — or expelled from it?"[10] The expulsion from the garden Tannen imagines, however, required the erection of a complete fictional framework, interesting and amusing. But if the advertisement is read in terms of mythic association, the message is clear and needs no literary fantasy.

In 1994 CLARINS introduced a new fragrance name ELYSIUM. It appeared in a pale sky blue bottle with white cloud swirl, and was given the motto "Heaven on Earth." The advertisements were simple and remained so: the bottle and its name dominated the page; a translucent bouquet of undefined flowers appeared as a shadow of the back-lit bottle.

No attempt was made to define the scent further; the name and the motto were to carry its message. Elysium is, of course, an ancient name for the afterworld's blessed islands; one does not need to delve deep into classical mythology to know this. Whether or not the ancients conceived of it as heaven on earth is open to speculation, for to them the realm of the dead was either beyond the limits of the known world, in the distant west (according to Homer's tale), or to be reached via a miraculous journey that began with a descent to Hades (as Vergil reports). Plato alone seemed to think that the realm of the blessed was accessible through the sky, although his description in the Myth of Er, in *Republic* Book X, is

---

[9] Mary Tannen, "The Biography of a Fragrance," in "Fashions of the Times," New York *Times* Magazine Part 2 (Fall, 1998): 70/74.

[10] Tannen further notes the appearance in 1996 of "White Linen Breeze," which she calls the daughter of White Linen. Is this an echo of Demeter and Persephone? But Tannen closes her "biography" of the fragrance by suggesting that the close relationship between mythic mother and daughter is not to be found in the modern world: "Considering the stiff competition in the fragrance world today...you would both be wise to watch your backs."

not easily imagined. Nevertheless, the idea of Elysium as a realm of the blessed (dead) is one commonly known.

With Clarin's new fragrance, apparently one does not need to die to experience the bliss of this happy realm; just wearing the perfume will transport its wearer to a more exalted and happier realm. This perfume, according to its initial advertisements, allows each user to achieve her own personal happiness, her heaven as she defines it.

When Karl Lagerfeld launched his perfume SUN MOON STARS early in 1995, the advertisements appeared to draw inspiration from the goddess associated with the moon, Selene, and this seemed appropriate.[11] The accompanying slogan was "to hold the sun moon stars in the palm of your hand..." The scent was marketed in a round blue bottle with the three heavenly figures worked into it and a golden globe formed the top. But it was model who accompanied the image and sentence that elevated the new aroma to mythological status.

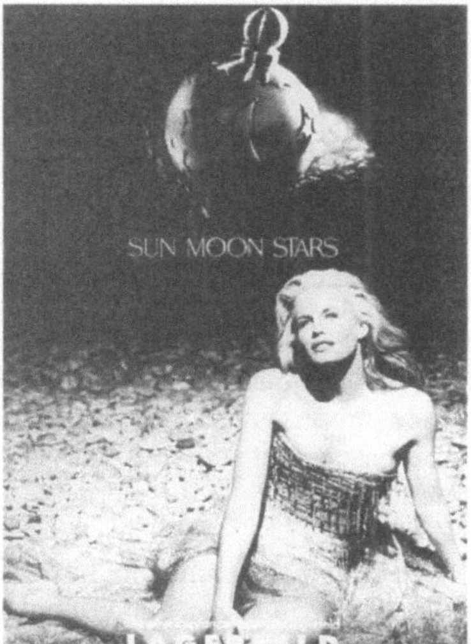

4.4 Karl Lagerfeld: *Sun Moon Stars*

The blond blue-eyed model was seated on a surface formed of small flat stones of the sort bordering lakes or forming many Mediterranean beaches, although the silvery blue lighting was clearly intended to represent a moonscape The woman was attired in a silver bare shouldered dress, with a skirt of fine netting flowing from the stretch bead-adorned bodice and spreading to form a coverlet on which she sat. She was gazing upwards as if seeing the moon and stars even as she herself represented them. Although the name included the three celestial aspects, only the moon and stars were emphasized in the

[11] The advertisement ran for several months in many magazines, including *ELLE* (November, 1994).

advertisements. Lagerfeld's initial illustration became clearly fixed in the public mind, his new fragrance promised its wearer thepower to hold Sun Moon and Stars in one's hand and share in the excitement and power generated by such an experience.

In the fall of that year, however, Lagerfeld altered the promotional image.[12] In the second in his advertising series for this perfume he depicted a woman emerging from a placid sea. Although we see only her head and shoulders exposed she is clearly unclothed. Her hair is damp, any makeup is virtually invisible: she is a part of the sea from which she is arising. A light shining in the background sky casts a gleaming path across the water; the dark and mysterious tone of the picture suggests the light comes from the moon, it is not the dawn sunrise illuminating the silent sea. This woman reflects the Aphrodite-from-the-sea trope; she seems to be one more in the perfume-and-goddess of love series. Did Lagerfeld choose to use the common cliché to promote this particular perfume? The scent's name allows him to be different, to break away from the familiar mythology and offer his audience something new. As the woman who could easily be identified as Selene was an apt illustration to introduce his new SUN MOON STARS, it stands to reason to continue the mythological reference. If one remembers that Selene arises from the sea each night, the image works. Lagerfeld's woman-from-the-sea is not the goddess "born of the sea-foam" but the divinity bringing on the night. Like PARFUMES CHLOÈ's *Narcisse*, Lagerfeld's SUN MOON STARS inhabits its own mythological realm.

During the fall of 1994 and spring of 1995, Princess Marcella Borghese, Inc. ran promotions for its CURA NOTTE and HYDROXY DI NOTTE COMPLEX (both of Borghese Trademarks, Inc), which while not perfumes are certainly intended for a woman's toilette. The advertisement depicted a line- drawing of a slip of new moon with a woman reclining within its arc.[13] The caption of the ads was "The Essence of Italian Beauty." The images were white and grey on a navy star-studded page.

The drawing sketched in the essence of Italian beauty: the woman, lean and dark-haired, wore a slacks suit with a deep-V neck, at the base of which was tied a

---

[12] The advertisement appeared in numerous magazines, including *Vanity Fair* (November, 1995).

[13] This advertisement appeared many times in many magazines, including *Vogue* (October, 1994).

large bow. This image played to our knowledge of classical mythology. For while in common modern parlance one speaks of "the man in the moon," the ancient Greeks and Romans considered the moon to be associated with a female divinity, Selene, who was herself later superseded by Artemis/ Diana.[14] As all divinities were by their very nature beautiful, any woman associated with the goddess of the moon would also be so. Here the "essence of Italian beauty" reflected the beauty of the moon-goddess: two standards of beauty would be met by the woman using CURA NOTTE carefully at night.

MONTEIL introduced a new fragrance in late 1995 and gave it a very simple name, *L'Eau de Monteil.* To promote this new scent, a light and delicate aroma reflecting the simplicity of its name, the company broke away from the familiar woman-in-sea image and chose to place its model in a leaf-shaded fresh water pool.[15] The young woman, pictured with damp hair and no apparent makeup, is submerged to her shoulders in the clear water. She has a dreamy look, intended, perhaps, to show how the refreshing quality of the water and the perfume transports its wearer away from ordinary concerns. The only text: The New Flagrance from MONTEIL. Paris.

On the second page of the advertisement we see a leaf-adorned bottle with the name of the scent. It, too, has been placed in cool clear green water, and the same large leaves shade its secluded place. Behind both the woman andthe bottle the pool flows into an indistinct darkness. The impression is of peaceful isolation: no cares can intrude upon this almost sacred place, a place of calm beauty into which this fragrance wafts its wearer. But there is more: myths of all cultures suggest that such pools are the abodes of divinities, albeit lesser ones; there are nymphs of rivers, streams and ponds. In a hot country such as Greece it is not strange that water spots were held to be holy, that a sense of powerful mystery surrounded places of such verdant beauty. Perhaps the model is not a mere woman after all. MONTEIL's advertisement suggests that the wearer of this scent may become a part of the magical world water nymphs inhabit.

---

[14] *Selene* was and still is a regular Greek word for moon (although demotic Greek commonly uses *phenggari* for it). As the early Titans were overthrown by the incoming Olympians, the old divinities yielded (per force) their realms of power to the new gods. Thus as Helios took over the guidance of the sun from Hyperion, so Artemis/Diana took over the realm of Selene.

[15] Among other places, the advertisement appeared in *Mademoiselle* (June, 1995).

Sea nymphs and mermaids permeate the world of perfumes, bath oils, and sunning creams, as they naturally suggest the healing power of the sea and the magic associated with it. In the 1990s, for example, Bain de Soleil challenged the sun with a very long-tailed mermaid perched on a rock. The model is deeply bronzed (surprisingly for a product claiming to ban the sun's rays!) but the implication is that even a sea nymph can endure long hours in the sun if she has applied Bain de Soleil.

The Earth Goddess, Mother Earth, or Gaea as she is called in Greek, was the earliest divinity to appear in the void of the early universe. From her were born many of the physical elements of the world, as were several abstract ideas, such as Justice and Fate and Righteousness. There were shrines to the Earth Goddess in many parts of the Greek landscape, and even when sanctuaries were taken over by the male Olympians, Zeus, Apollo and others, Gaea never went without recognition. Nor has she faded from modern thought.

Mother Earth, Mother Nature, is referred to by many people, casually, perhaps, but at some level the oft quoted phrase, "It's not nice/safe to anger Mother Nature" remains a belief. So the Earth Goddess appears to advertise various products, she is invoked to promote items of many types.

Willow Lake, creator of "soothing shampoos and conditioners made from flowers and herbs" designed an advertisement that plays off the company name and Mother Nature. In the June 1997 promotions we see a woman's head and torso emerging from water, presumably Willow Lake. The text invites: "Come to Wllow Lake and let Earth mother your hair." The divinity's name has become a verb, but the allusion is clear. The various flowers and herbs that have been combined in Willow Lake products would seem to rely upon the alchemy of Mother Nature: Cherry Bark & Irish Moss blend for one conditioner, Witch Hazel and Honey-suckle for a shampoo. Advertisement, name and product arise from popular belief in an ancient divinity who seems to still have power.

Mythological allusions underlined most perfume advertisements of the 1990s, but occasionally the simple "classic" idea served to add status to a scent. When Givenchy launched its new luxury perfume in 1998, it designed a bottle that evoked both a classic column and the name of the perfume, *Organza*.[16] Inside a clear shaft a fluted feminine form holds the scent; the bottle top is a reversed Ionic

[16] Advertisements for the new perfume were to be found in every magazine, including *Glamour* (October, 1998).

capital. In the advertisement's illustration, a woman stands next to a life-sized bottle, clad in a white pleated/fluted organza gown that repeats the vial's shape and flows into a spreading column base at her feet. Statuesque and striking, the woman as bottle gains class from the reflection of ancient architecture. *Organza*'s name is not classic, but the gold and white advertisement for it certainly is.

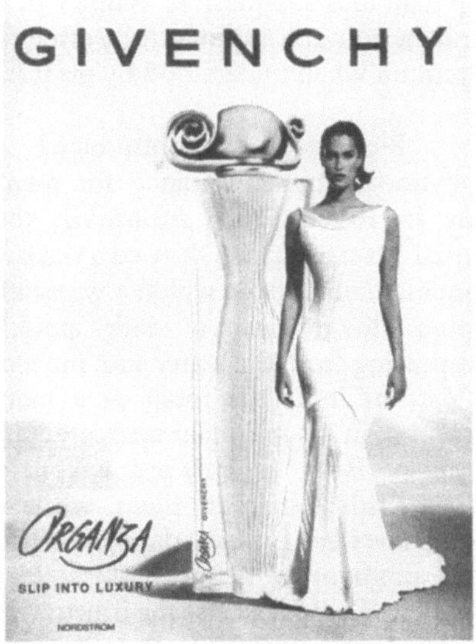

4.5 Givenchy: *Organza*

Fragrances for Men

Classical allusions are not limited to the feminine world. Ancient gods and their powers animate the advertisements for many articles for men as well: clothing, accessories, and fragrances. The latter ads especially take inspiration from Greek and Roman figures. Unlike women's lines, however, men's fashions and scents look to the classical for advertising copy but not for names. Women's wear and perfumes are often named Artemis or Venus, but men's products for the most part (there are some exceptions) take simple direct names and rely on the illustration to provide the mythic reference and hence meaning.

In the early 1990s Coty introduced *Gravity* cologne for men. With the caption "More than a fragrance It's a force of nature" the cologne was illustrated with a man and woman sinking into an embrace by a rocky seacoast. Or have they arisen from the dark purple-banded triangle that fills the lower third of the page? This advertisement for *Gravity*, subheaded "You couldn't resist it, even if you tried" is apparently directed to the woman as she meets a man wearing the fragrance. The picture thus suggests the Hades and Persephone story: rising from the underworld, this strong and handsome man will carry the fainting woman back to his realm. Yet a quiet calm pervades the picture, so that the man and woman appear to illustrate a *hieros gamos,* a holy marriage, a marriage between heaven and earth. The second page of the advertisement, however, asserts that "There isn't a man on earth who can resist a gift of gravity." Suddenly the power changes hands: it is the woman who seduces the man with her irresistible pull, it is the dangerous female who draws the man into submission. While Coty probably merely wished the shopper would find the cologne as powerfully attractive as its name, the illustration draws far more attention when understood by mythic reference.

Pierre Cardin introduced a "passionate new fragrance for men" late in 1995. Called *Insatiable*, the initial advertisements showed a verdant mountain cliff, from which a waterfall pours down into a dark pool.[17] Appearing from the water and, indeed, a part of it, is the torso of a man, grasping in his muscular arms a young woman. Both figures are naked; a silvery mist encircles them, while a brilliance rises from the dark pool. This is a moment of mystery as well as passion. The text across the illustration is brief and powerful: Drench your body. Drench her soul.

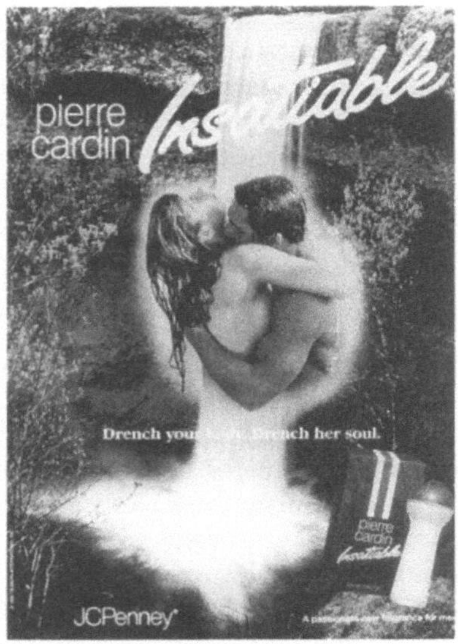

4.6 Pierre Cardin: *Insatiable*

The picture, drenched with sexuality, is also laden with mythological suggestions. Many a legend tells of a young woman seized by a water god: rivers, streams and fountains had their resident deity and these, both male and female, were amorous gods. Here the green mountainside setting implies that the image arises from the common idea of divinity residing within the river or stream. Thus while Pierre Cardin has chosen no particular myth to carry his message, the various tales are so familiar that one need not be specified. The man who has drenched his body in the flowing fragrance of *Insatiable* will easily capture both body and soul of any young woman. The man who wears *Insatiable* will find his desire satisfied as he totally possesses its object.

As so many manufacturers of a clothing line have done, JOOP! offered an eau de toilette in 1995, and titled it NIGHTFLIGHT.[18] Its blue bottle was

[17] The advertisement appeared in many magazines, including *Vogue* (October, 1995).

[18] NIGHTFLIGHT advertisements appeared (with an offer of a phonecard) in many of the major magazines, including *Glamour* (September, 1995) and *Elle* (November, 1995).

emblazoned with airplanes, but the advertisement pictured a man's muscular body posed dramatically against a star's point. The figure bends backwards, bracing his right arm and leg against the star; he is standing on his left leg and his left arm is bent back across his body so that his hand touches his right shoulder. What image is this?

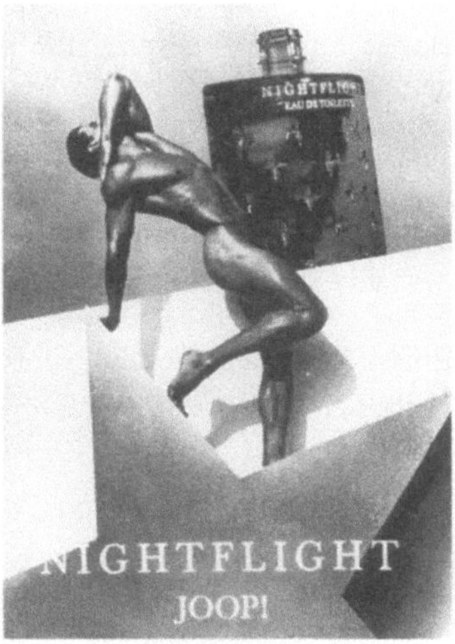

4.7 Jonbil: *Joop! Nightflight*

Several possibilities come to mind. The figure could be just an unnamed athlete, of course, but his stance appears to have been deliberately chosen. Prometheus, the mighty Titan, benefactor of mankind, comes to mind, but no myth associates this character with flight. Adonis, the most beautiful of mythological figures and the possible inspiration for other masculine advertisements, e.g. the Davidoff colognes COOL WATER and ZINO (see Chapter III), neither flies nor flexes his muscles. More likely candidates are Daedalus or Icarus. But the latter, although known for his flight, is better known for his fall, and thus would be singularly inappropriate for a cologne named flight. Daedalus stands as a very good option. The clever inventor successfully designed wings for flight; any mortal who can fly must have been physically fit. The stance of the model suggests the moment before he takes wing: poised against the star, he will throw back his bent arm and vault into the air. Daedalus' association with invention makes him an appropriate figure for JOOP!, for, as we have seen, it is a brand name identified with inspiring thoughtful reflection.

JOOP! wants the buyer to ponder the possibilities of this cologne which promises "an explosion of freshness." The striking image increases the promotional illustration's appeal when pondered in terms of mythic association. NIGHTFLIGHT from JOOP! attracts attention even as do the jeans the company designs. Color and image enhance what the name can suggest and, in the promotion of cologne or perfume, the success of the product rests on the image presented in the advertisement.

JOOP!'s commercial is aimed directly at the male shopper. In 1965, a different time, advertisements for men's products were directed to the one who frequented the stores, the woman of the house. When Elizabeth Arden came out with her *Classic Cologne* for men (formulated in Italy "where they understand what appeals to men"), the lead-in line on its advertisement was "A Latin touch for your lover." The text played off a woman's teasing of her man: Drop a package in his Christmas stocking, she was advised: "He'll think you did it for him, but Elizabeth Arden really did it for you." What Italians know "appeals to men" also by implication appeals to women. To underscore the scent's name, box and bottle were adorned with an image of a horseman taken from a Greek vase painting.

WOMEN'S ATTIRE

Clothing, as we noted in Chapter II, has long been promoted via classical allusion. The association of the Classic and attire has not faded. Talbots, for example, rests its reputation on making "classic" clothes and its simply illustrated advertisements gain their power from a series of different definitions of classic: "Classic is...." In the spring of 1994, *Vogue*'s fashion editors collected a series of dresses for the season presented under the title "a Grecian turn":

> This season designers celebrate an ancient rite of
> spring. Inspired by nymphs, goddesses and Isadora
> Duncan, they've created simple, sweetly wanton dresses
> with romantic drapery....[19]

The flimsy fabrics draped models in various woodland scenes who were identified as "a nineties goddess," "a little lost tree nymph," and "Artemis, goddess of the hunt;" the last model aims a prop bow & arrow, while her short dress abounds with extra cloth so as to look like the tucked-up tunic of the Grecian goddess. The modern nymphs of spring in their innocent poses exude sexuality, an aura and

[19] *Vogue* (May, 1994): 266-275. The photographs were by Ellen Von Unwerth; the dresses were from many designers, including Karl Lagerfeld, Chloè, and Holly Lueders.

attitude that would have expelled them from the coterie of the fiercely virginal Artemis. But the conceit is attractive, the concept appealing. The fashion rites of spring in the *Vogue* collection is far different from the "Classic is..." designs of Talbot or other clothiers who turn to antiquity for inspiration, but their power comes from the same source.

In an advertisement running in February, 1994, GUESS? portrayed a young woman hoeing in a rice paddy.[20] She is clad in tall boots, thigh-high (but no higher) dark stockings, short shorts, a dark deeply cut tight-fitting sweater that leaves the midriff bare, while a scarf covers and ties back her light colored hair. This outfit could be worn in any of a number of settings: a hike on the beach or in a meadow, at a barbecue, even while reclining on a porch swing (although there the boots might be unnecessary). Thus we must consider just why GUESS chose to put their model in to an agricultural setting, into the producing of a staple grain.[21]

Mythology once again offers at least one answer. Although the model is young, goddesses are traditionally ageless, and thus she can represent an earth deity: a figure involved in the tending of the soil, responsible for its fertility and its success in offering a basic food for human consumption. Demeter or Ceres was the grain goddess; she sent forth Triptolemus to teach the planting of crops, while she herself made sure the earth produced each year. Her daughter Persephone was also involved in crop cultivation. Persephone's most famous story is that of her abduction by Hades and her subsequent return to the upper world, a return that signaled the spring rebirth of the seasons, but certain aspects of the rituals associated withher, as well as pure "logic," suggest that she shared with her mother a concern for mortal well-being. Thus GUESS?s well-endowed hard working rice-field laborer can be viewed as a goddess in charge of the fertility and productivity of the land: either Demeter herself or Persephone her daughter.

If we follow this line of reasoning, then we can assume that the wearer of GUESS? attire is working for the common good of the human race. It may indicate that the woman who wears GUESS? clothing thereby ensures fertility of the crops, but I suspect the advertisement's creator had the larger perspective in mind. We are to see the GUESS? model as laboring to make the world a better place, a place

---

[20] Among other places, this advertisement appeared in *Vogue* (February, 1994).

[21] Every effective advertisement will recall different images for each viewer. This woman-in-the-rice-field could allude to a familiar film or photograph. The identification of an ad's classical roots, by offering meaning as well visual recollection, increases its power.

where famine is unknown and no child goes to bed hungry. Great is the power of GUESS? garments.

Over the years numerous articles of women's apparel have been named and/or promoted with classical names: lingerie, shoes, handbags and bathing suits have been designated by ancient deities. Artemis has been especially popular for lingerie, goddess of arts and crafts Athena/Minerva for shoes (sandals or pumps), Dionysus for jewelry and nails (an interesting thought!) and, of course, Aphrodite/Venus for just about everything, while classical columns frame every product a woman would wish to buy. The modern American shopper moves and purchases in a world pervaded by echoes of ancient Greece and Rome.[22]

MEN'S WEAR

In the fall of 1994 GUESS? came out with an advertisement for its Men's Classics modeled closely on a traditional theme but with a modern twist.[23] A young man, attired in a plaid GUESS flannel shirt stands before us. Held on his shoulders is a black dog, lightly powdered with snow. No words other than the brand name appear in the ad. The man's earnest expression reveals him to be a sensitive person; his careful grip on the dog show he is also one who shows concern for his fellow creatures. The dog seems to realize his good deed.

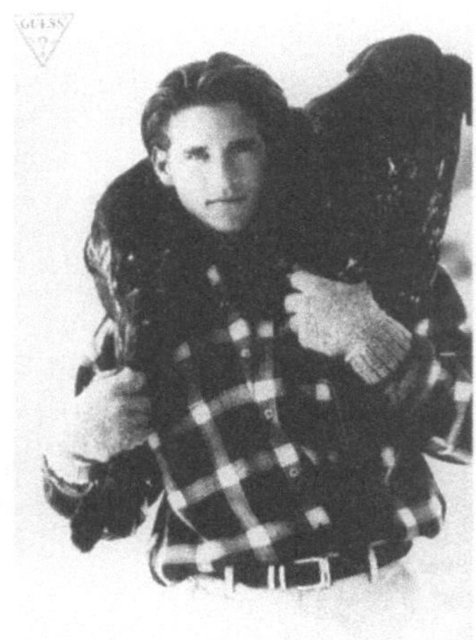

4.8 Guess?: Shirt

[22]The classical world flourishes in European advertisements as well where name and illustration alike are also taken from ancient Greece and Rome. This study can only look at ads on this side of the Atlantic.

[23] This advertisement appeared in many magazines, including *Vogue* (November, 1994).

The picture was appropriate for the Christmas season, for its roots go back to illustrations of Christ as Good Shepherd. In early Christian iconography, Christ is frequently portrayed, both in plastic and painted/mosaic arts, holding a lamb as the young man in the GUESS advertisement holds the dog. The wearer of GUESS clothing is a devout and caring person.

The portrayal of Christ as Good Shepherd can be traced to an earlier period. One of the best known statues from the archaic period of Greek sculpture is the *Moschophoros*, the Calf-bearer. The statue now stands in the Acropolis Museum in Athens; the figure's expression, although in archaic calm, clearly shows his devotion to his deity. It is this image that the early Christian iconographers borrowed when depicting Jesus Christ as pastor of His flock.

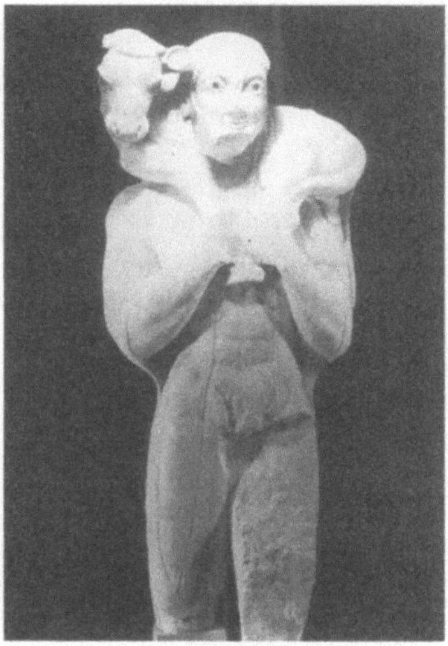

4.9 Moschophoros(Calf-Bearer). Athens \ Acropolis Museum

There is, however, an important difference between the archaic Greek statue and the illustrations of the Christian iconographers. The *Moschophoros* stands devoutly before his divinity *with his appropriate offering*: the calf will be his sacrificial victim. Within the dictates of ancient Greek cult, the reverent individual offers to the god a most perfect animal; thus does he show his true devotion. Christ as good shepherd protects his flock for its benefit; the Moschophoros tends his to provide for the gods.

Surely the creator of the GUESS? advertisement drew his inspiration from the early Christian images: the model for the flannel shirt has saved his dog. But by the echo of the classical statue, a new layer of meaning has been added. The wearer of GUESS? classic clothes, posed as a classic statue,is devout, yes, but is his an act of salvation or of sacrifice? We are left to wonder, but which ever act is intended, there is no doubt but that by wearing GUESS? attire we will know the right thing to do.

While not as extreme as the "Just A Thought!" series run by JOOP!, in that the models in the GUESS? ads are in fact wearing some clothing made by the company, still there is no single direction given to the potential audience as to the ad's meaning or to buy the attire. Thus GUESS? advertisements permit the viewer to create a meaning, and to do that the viewer must bring to play his/her cultural awareness. The advertisements that encourage men and women to buy GUESS? clothing suggest that the wearer of this line will be a part of society's larger concerns, be a better citizen of a world wherein they will take correct and compassionate action.

Jackson Lears analyzed the power of advertisements in his seminal study, *Fables of Abundance. A Cultural History of Advertising in America.* In its opening pages he suggests:

> During the last two hundred years, in the capitalist West and increasingly elsewhere as well, advertisements have acquired a powerful iconic significance. Yet they have been more than static symbols: they have coupled words and pictures in commercial fables- stories that have been both fabulous and didactic, that have evoked fantasies and pointed morals, that have reconfigured ancient dreams of abundance to fit the modern world of goods. By the late twentieth century, these fables of abundance-especially the ones sponsored by major multinational corporations- had become perhaps the most dynamic and sensuous representations of cultural values in the world.[24]

In its 1994 advertisements the GUESS? company participates in this sensual representation of cultural values. The maker of stylish clothes proves it has a social conscience. By its advertisements the company promotes its product and its image.

Z. Cavaricci, manufacturer of designer sports clothes, changes its advertisements frequently; each month a different image is offered, and, indeed, different images in different magazines during the same month. In March, 1995, two advertisements were published, each different, but both drew inspiration from classical sources. Both ads were inscribed in a circle of flowing script with the motto: "Suppress no urge."

The advertisement appearing in *Rolling Stone* (23 March, 1995) recalled the story of Pygmalion, the artist who fell in love with his work. In a studio cluttered with bits and pieces of classical molding, an artist stands beside a model on a

---

[24] Jackson Lears, *Fables of Abundance. A Cultural History of Advertising in America.* (New York: Basic Books, 1994):2.

pedestal. He looks out at us, having just finished sculpting his ideal woman; the final wood shavings are at her feet. She, partially draped in a cloth in the manner familiar from numerous ancient statues, is turned away from him and us, but she is clearly living flesh. A golden light suffuses the whole; only the artist's red apron and the purple lettering of the motto break the picture's golden hues.

The sole article of clothing in the entire picture, apart from the sculptor's apron, is his (golden) jeans: are these the item to be purchased? What message is Z. Cavaricci presenting? Classical legend helps the viewer to understand the advertisement better; the story of Pygmalion (as told above in Chapter II) illustrates the message. The Greek artist who came to love the statue he was sculpting and prayed she might be given life had his prayer answered by Aphrodite: when he returned to his studio he found that his statue came alive under his touch. Pygmalion's story became part of western culture's mythology; from ancient Greece to the present time, the artist who falls in love with his work is described in terms of this story.

Z. Cavaricci's depiction reaches us at several levels. The sculptor is a creator of fine things, his handiwork animates the inanimate. The creator of Z. Cavaricci's designer clothes offers the potential wearer artistic power; so attired one can create vital works of art. The motto recalls Pygmalion's daring prayer, his plea that his marble maiden be granted life. It might also refer to his self-admission of his love for his statue; in either case he had suppressed no urge. Finally, the entire advertisement, based on a myth which is only visually expressed, elevates the viewer who understands into the circle of those who know. The wearer of Z. Cavaricci's clothes, we are to understand, is part of the educated elite, a person whose cultural heritage is intact and thus familiar with the mythology of western art and literature. Z. Cavaricci's *Rolling Stone* advertisement encloses the magazine's readers into the circle of the *cognoscenti*.

Also appearing in March, 1995, but in other magazines, was a different advertisement for Z. Cavaricci's clothes.[25] The image was different, but the message was equally indirect. Here a young woman (of natural proportion- not the starved models of, e.g., Calvin Klein) crouches on a bronzed pedestal. She holds a lit electric light bulb dangling from a wire, its cord not visibly plugged in at all. In its illumination she looks out at us while we look at her denim shorts, held up by suspenders over a striped knit top. Again, the motto "Suppress no urge" is inscribed in script around the figure, this time in light grey.

[25] The advertisements appeared in *Glamour* and *Elle* (March, 1995).

What message is being given? The young woman appears to be guiding us with her light, guiding the potential buyer to a purchase of Z. Cavaricci's clothes. But other images might have conveyed this idea more clearly. Thus again we must look to our knowledge of ancient myth to interpret this advertisement correctly.

The best-known feminine guide of antiquity was Ariadne, the Minoan princess who led Theseus through the maze of the labyrinth to his contest with the Minotaur, the half-man, half-bull lurking at the center of the palace of Knossos on the island of Crete. The ancient Ariadne, of course, used a ball of twine. But a gleaming electric light bulb has become part of the artistic tradition associated with the myth for she is thus portrayed in Picasso's grand painting of the story. In the modern artist's canvas, Ariadne raises on high a single light bulb to illuminate the Minotaur and his conqueror. Thus in Z. Cavaricci's rendition, "Ariadne" appears to guide us through the maze of competing brands and styles, and offers us a way to conquer the labyrinth of fashion. If we know the story, we know its successful outcome, and thus we can follow the model's guiding light to a safe and proper conclusion.

There is an interesting aspect to this "Ariadne" advertisement: it seems to be related to the Pygmalion ad, for the two seem to share common elements. Perhaps the similarity arises simply from a dual use of studio props and models, but if the two images are examined closely together, two things can be noticed. First, the pedestal in both ads is very similar, although color and camera angle mask this to the casual observer. Second, the models themselves look alike. One we see from the back, the other faces us, but build, hairstyle and hair ornament are much alike. Since the legend of Pygmalion and his lady, sometimes called Galatea, and that of Ariadne and Theseus are not part of the same cycle, I don't think we are to see a mythic connection between the two advertisements. I do think, however, that we are to interpret the two from the same vantage point: from our knowledge of western myth we can understand the advertisements' message. As part of that circle of those who are educated in western culture's literature and art, we are those who will appreciate the creations of Z. Cavaricci.

Z.Cavaricci's ads in the summer of 1995 take a different approach. In July's magazines we do not need to know myth to understand the message.[26] The man wearing the jeans sits on the edge of a bronzed old-fashioned bathtub, holding a slim book (probably poetry), while his lady basksin a bubble bath with high-class

[26] The advertisement appeared in such magazines as *Elle* and *Cosmopolitan* (July, 1995).

hardback books beside her; her Z. Cavaricci jeans are on the floor. His wrist is tattooed with an intricate design while his shoulder boasts the brand name. Here the message, still unstated, is more clear: the wearer of Z. Cavaricci's clothes now leads a comfortable life, surrounded by literature and appreciative of beauty. Those of us who purchase these clothes are still part of the inner circle of the better classes, but we do not need to know mythology to understand the advertisement's message.

DRIVING WITH CLASS: AUTOMOBILES ENHANCED BY CLASSICAL ASSOCIATION

The automobile, a basic means of transportation now available to almost everyone in America, has long stood in American culture as an object of self-expression and self-evaluation. The family car, the sports car, the van and the RV each reflect a certain life style as well as social status.[27] Whichever vehicle suits an individual's way of life and self-image, the advertisements that define that vehicle play a very important role in defining the vehicle's owner.

In the ads of the 1990s the car is seldom seen, in print media, as being a car, that is, offering smooth efficient transportation. True, motion cannot be actually represented in a static illustration, but a suggestion of movement is possible. Even in television commercials, the contemporary car is seldom seen in a real-life situation. It is shown dashing through isolated territory to an even more isolated destination, finally parked on a lonely

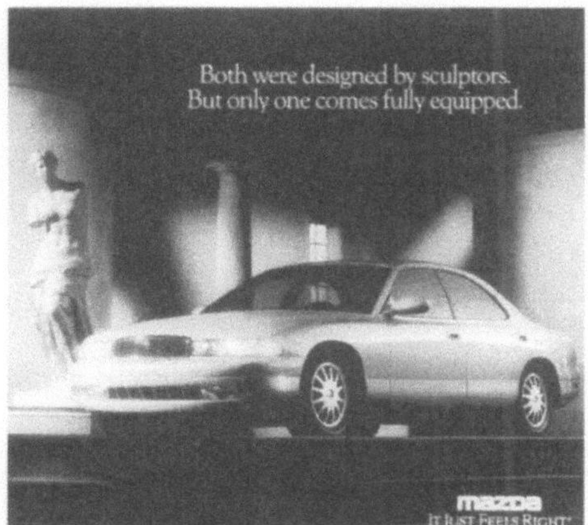

4.10 Mazda

[27] Andrew Wernick, *Promotional Culture*, writes (70), that "Cars,..are similar to clothes, constituting indeed a kind of third skin for ambient industrial man." Wernick devotes a chapter of his book to cars and the technological image they represent in current (1980s) American society.

peak.[28] The print media car, however, is portrayed as an *objet d 'art*, gracing a fine mansion. To give real class to an automobile via its advertisement, a Greek or Roman statue or some Ionic columns are added to indicate that as these ancient artifacts have class so does the modern automobile. The Venus di Milo is a thing of beauty, so is a new MAZDA, and thus it is shown parked before a column, sharing a platform with a copy of the Venus di Milo.[29] Similarly, Acura's advertisement, showing the car flanked by a series of classic statues, such as the discus thrower and an Artemis, needed no descriptive text to explain its meaning.[30] This Acura parked between two Ionic columns illustrates the lasting beauty of the car in a way that placing it on a green hillside or in a western park could not.[31] Television advertisements for cars can show the vehicle speeding through a beautiful landscape, but in print media the message must be carried by a static image. What better way exists to telegraph a car's enduring class than to juxtapose it to a familiar and commonly accepted icon of value, or within a setting quickly recognized as "classic"?

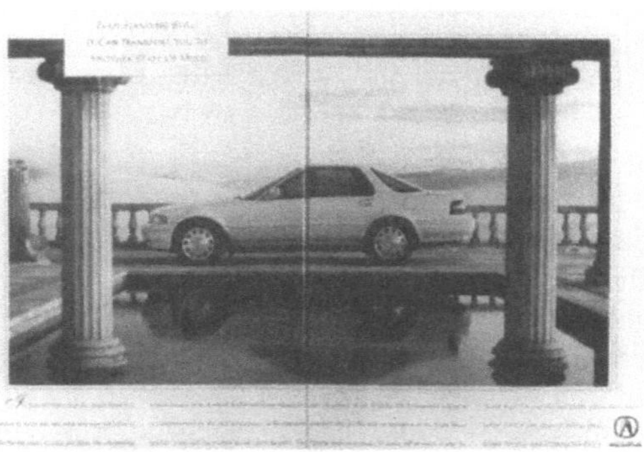

4.11 Acura

[28] Two exceptions could be cited: the car (driven 90% of the time by a woman) is moving along a wet, dark and dangerous road or the van (again, usually driven by a woman, "the soccer mom") is shown transporting numbers of children and pets to some venue of entertainment.

[29] Among other places, the Venus di Milo MAZDA advertisement appeared in *Gourmet* (November, 1994), with text "Both were designed by sculptors. But only one comes fully equipped."

[30] Advertisement of the spring 1995 campaign, appearing, among other places, in *Gourmet* (March 1995).

[31] Advertisement appeared in many magazines, including *Esquire* (April, 1994).

MYTHOLOGY AROUND THE HOUSE

Poseidon, god of the sea and second brother of Zeus does not appear as frequently in modern advertisements as one might suppose. In ancient myth he commanded great respect from the sea-bounded Greeks. Along the rocky Aegean coast many temples were built for this deity who controlled waves and earthquakes, two constantly threatening dangers of the Greek naturalworld. Only some of these temples still stand, as that on the promontory at Sunion, for example, on whose columns Lord Byron once carved his name. But the evidence for many others remains in the columns, standing beside or rebuilt into numerous chapels along the Greek coast today, chapels dedicated to Saint Nicholas, the successor to the ancient marine deity.

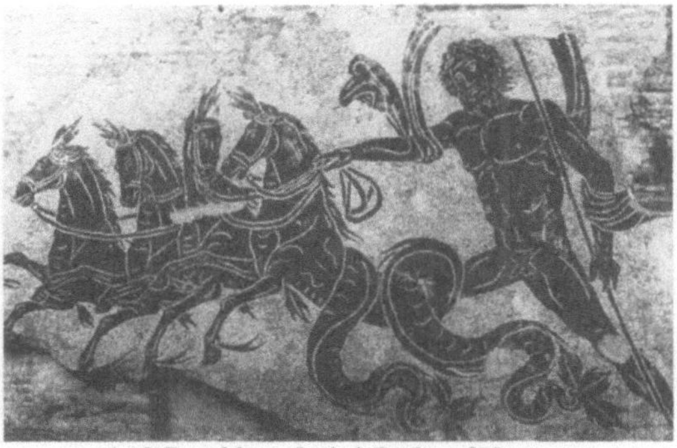

4.12 Poseidon. Ostia \ Baths of Neptune

It was believed that Poseidon had turned up the islands of Greece with his trident, his tool when doing such constructive work, his weapon when angered by those who boasted they could master the waves. Ancient artists portrayed Poseidon driving over the waves a chariot pulled by horses with serpentine tails and heralded by Tritons, sea-men who blew shell trumpets. At times his wife Amphitrite accompanied him, as in the famous fresco from Piazza Amerina in Sicily. But more frequently the deity dashed alone across the waves, holding his trident at the ready, with his cloak arching out behind him.

Poseidon was a divinity to be carefully propitiated. And when Aeolus, King of the Winds, worked with him, men at sea stood little chance of survival. Ancient literary descriptions of Poseidon's wrath are as evocative and memorable as the painted images. In the aftermath of his storm in Aeschylus' *Agamemnon*, for example, the sea is said to "blossom with corpses," (659) while his long-smouldering rage against Odysseus kept the hero away from Ithaca for many years.

As we have seen, KOHLER enlists ancient myth to promote its modern products. In the spring of 1994 the company turned to the god of the sea for its kitchen sink advertisements. "The Bold Look of KOHLER" promoted its Ballad stainless steel sinks with not one, but two, images drawn from ancient Greek divinities.[32] The text immediately asserts the source, although the deities are not named:

> Wanna make some real waves in your kitchen? Our Ballad
> stainless steel sinks have all the elements in their favor.
> Note the classic lines (ours have real character) in single, double, triple and bar sink styles. Now, how does that strike you?

The words "classic lines" point us to the drawing's theme, while the gods' powers are suggested by both "real character" and the lead in phrase, a phrase given in casual language to lessen any implied sense of exclusion by the assumed familiarity with the images. The closing sentence also neatly combines learned allusion and contemporary jargon.

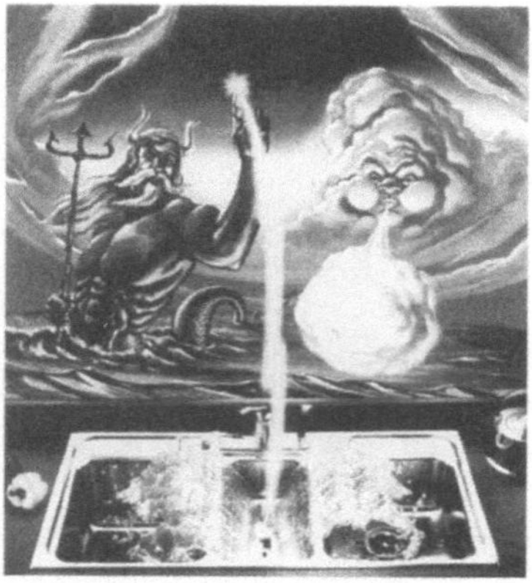

4.13 Kohler:
Ballad Sink

The illustration, #24 in the "As I See It" series, was created by John Walker, who titled it "It's All Greek to Me." Above a tri-part sink Poseidon rises on the left from a stormy sea. His right hand holds his trident, with his left index finger he sends a bolt of lightning into the sink's center, causing waves to splash over into the other basins. On the right Aeolus appears within a storm cloud, blowing a wind-filled cloud toward the sink; more waves will soon be created. The brilliant blues and greens of the illustration intensify the powerful forces of the divinities.

[32] The advertisement appeared in *Gourmet* (March, 1994).

While it is probably true that most housewives or other home cooks do *not* in fact want to make "real waves" in the kitchen, the advertisement is effective. By its allusions we understand that the person who stands at this sink will feel a sense of power, will realize her/his kitchen is a place of assertive creativity, all the while knowing the strength of KOHLER, allied with the ancient nature divinities of the classical world, are supporting work done there.

MYTHOLOGY & TOBACCO CIGARETTES

Banned from television advertising, cigarette companies fill the pages of popular magazines with promotions of their product. Some, like Marlboro and VIRGINIA SLIMS, have long marked out an identifying theme: Marlboro has a country, VIRGINIA SLIMS has come a long way. The figures of ancient myth do not appear in their commercials.

In recent years Philip Morris created an identifying realm for its *Parliament Lights,* a setting which subtly yet clearly evokes the islands of Greece. The men and women who choose to smoke Philip Morris do so on the terraces of starkly white buildings before a brilliant blue sea or sky. The architecture is simple, at times no more than a typical Greek island balcony, perhaps, at times a column recalls an ancient temple, an ambiance always suggestive of the cigarettes' subtext, "The Perfect Recess." The smokers are safely enclosed in their pure white and blue world. The illustration is modern and classical in its clean lines and style. While the advertisement does not rely upon any particular familiarity with the ancient world, it manages to establish the sense of value always associated with it.

BENSON & HEDGES (another Philip Morris cigarette) has always been promoted with intriguing and/or provocative advertisements. In 1995, when more and more places were banning inside smoking, the company introduced a series suggesting that smokers would go to any length or height for their pleasure. The settings for these people pursuing their smoke varied; at times they were on an airplane wing, on a point of Liberty's crown, or within a ship's lifeboat. In the later months of that year, the company chose to place its followers among the limbs of the gigantic figures forming a classical pediment on a public building.[33] Seated on the knee of Zeus, in the hand of a larger-than-life young man or leaning against his leg, small figures are doing their regular office work while enjoying a BENSON &

[33] The advertisement appeared in *GQ* (August, 1995) among many other places.

HEDGES. A large clock with Roman numerals in the center of the scene indicates the time to be ten minutes before two. The text above the eye-catching illustration reads:

> Today, trying to smoke in some public buildings is a monumental task. For a great smoke, just work it out.

The sculpture pedimental group represents any public building where more and more interior smoking is forbidden. The office workers who still enjoy their cigarettes have gathered together to find a suitable place, away from harassment, away from legal prohibitions. In this advertisement, the key word is "monumental," for the text suggests those who persist can find such a setting. These workers have "worked it out," they have found a place, against great odds, perhaps, to smoke. Beneath the impassive gaze of the ancient gods, they can enjoy their cigarettes.

While monumentality is the important idea, the choice of a classical facade is, perhaps, significant. The right to smoke is given a greater status by the implication that it is as much a part of modern culture as is neo-classical architecture. These heroic figures are not bothered by cigarette smoke. It is time to take a longer look, Philip Morris through their BENSON & HEDGES advertisement seems to imply, and to reconsider laws which force those who would smoke to go to such lengths to enjoy their cigarettes. The advertisement also suggests that for those who purchase BENSON & HEDGES, no task is too great.

"She's gone to Capri and she's not coming back." With this slogan and a variety of settings evocative of the Italian isle, the B & T Tobacco Company promotes its *Capri* Superslim cigarettes. While Capri is a definite location, there is a sense of timelessness and an aura of myth about each illustration.

The picture in the November 1995 advertisement shows a woman seated by a stone fountain.[34] The water tumbles and splashes behind her, pots of flowers adorn the encircling rim of the fountain's basin. She appears pensive, perhaps reflexive. A woman by a well could be associated with Demeter, stopping by the Kallichore Well at Eleusis, for the Earth Mother had rested at the well during her quest to find her lost daughter, Persephone, snatched down to the realm of the dead by Hades. But that is an unhappy story. *Capri*'s woman might rather be Hera, ready to bath in the waters of the Kanathos. This myth brings to mind ideas of purification and

[34] The advertisement appeared in all the standard magazines, including *Mademoiselle* (November, 1995).

rejuvenation. The queen of the gods, herself by succession in the earth mother tradition, bathed annually at this magical spring to restore her virginity. The *Capri* advertisement (while probably not following that tradition too closely!) can suggest that those who smoke these Superslims will find their youth restored; the B &T Tobacco company can intimate that their product has purifying qualities. If this advertisement is viewed in terms of myth, it gains in impact: to smoke *Capri* Superslims offers more than an escape to an Italian island, (a pleasure resort even for the Romans): to smoke these cigarettes offers both power and rejuvenation.

WINES & LIQUORS

Wine and liquor advertisements also turn to mythological themes to attract attention to their product. Johnnie Walker looked to the Pygmalion story for its early 1990s ads to promote its BLACK LABEL Scotch. The Pygmalion theme, used by Z. Cavaricci and by others (as we have seen) is especially popular in modern advertising, perhaps due to its familiarity via Shaw's script or the famous musical based upon it: Eliza Doolittle and Henry Higgins are household names. But recent ad makers have reversed the genders of the mythic figures. Now it is the woman who is the artist, it is her creation that comes to life.

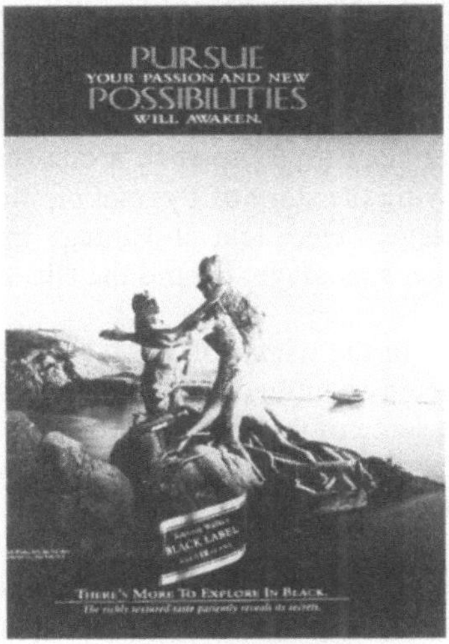

4.14 Johnnie Walker: *Black Label* Scotch

Thus in the fall of 1995 Johnnie Walker came out with an exotic advertisement for its Black Label Scotch.[35] An eerie seaside landscape is portrayed in copper tone, a scene wherein a low rock cliff comes down to a glass-calm sea and a rowboat, with oars still extended, rests at the wave line. Above this picture is printed the heading, "PURSUE your passion and new POSSIBILITIES will awaken." In the central foreground a young woman has been carving an isolated tree stump with many exposed roots into a male torso. At the moment captured in the ad's picture her

[35] The advertisement was in many magazines, including *Wired* (November, 1995).

statue seems to have come to life and extends an arm toward her. She herself has at that instant reached out to touch his hair, her hammer held lightly in her palm. While she may have carved his arm outstretched, the expression on her face and the animate bend of the male figure and his enfleshed arm reveal he has, indeed, awakened under her touch, her wooden image has come to life. Although the outstretched arm of each figure forbids an embrace at that moment, the message is clear: the artist has fallen in love with her work, her work has responded to her passion. The woman has pursued her art to this exotic and deserted cove and her passion has awakened her creation.

Beneath the pictured label there is further text. "There's More to Explore in Black. The richly textured taste patiently reveals its secrets." To the one who explores its taste the whiskey will open its hidden core. Such will be the reward of the one who drinks Johnnie Walker's Black Label. Without rowing to a deserted coast the Scotch drinker can bring her/his work to life. The adventure lies in the consumption, the results are waiting to awaken.

The advertisement's message is without meaning for one who does not know the ancient myth; to such a one the ad's picture can only seem strange. But by knowing the story of Pygmalion the viewer of this advertisement understands its message. Here text and image interact in the field of myth to carry Johnnie Walker's message: behind the Black Label life has fuller significance.

In the winter of 1993-1994, CHIVAS REGAL offered an advertisement that attracted attention by the fact that the image had nothing to do with whisky at all. Like some of the clothing ads that show no picture of the advertised garment, the liquor company compelled the viewer to look again: what does a mermaid on an isolated rocky coast have to do with blended Scotch whiskey?[36]

The answer lay in the accompanying text: "As long as there are stories about the one that got away... There will always be a CHIVAS REGAL." The ad's creator was playing off a number of familiar images which he combined in a new way to put forth the company's message. Sports fishermen will always be telling about the one they almost caught-everyone knows that. So as people do not change, so the quality and taste of CHIVAS REGAL will not change. But "the one that got away" always refers to a fish, not a mermaid, for even the most consummate liar and the

---

[36] Among other places, the advertisement appeared in *U.S. News and World Report* (January 24, 1994).

most gullible listener will not believe the elusive catch was a fair, salmon - tailed sea maid.

But a picture of a fish, no matter how grand, would send an message entirely different from that suggested by the beautiful mermaid reclining on her lonely rocks.[37] A real fish would appeal to another type of audience, one that may or may not drink CHIVAS REGAL. On the other hand, to suggest that those who enjoy this brand of Scotch whiskey might spot a mermaid adds an element of mystery and excitement that would appeal to anyone who sails the sea, involved in either sports or commercial fishing.

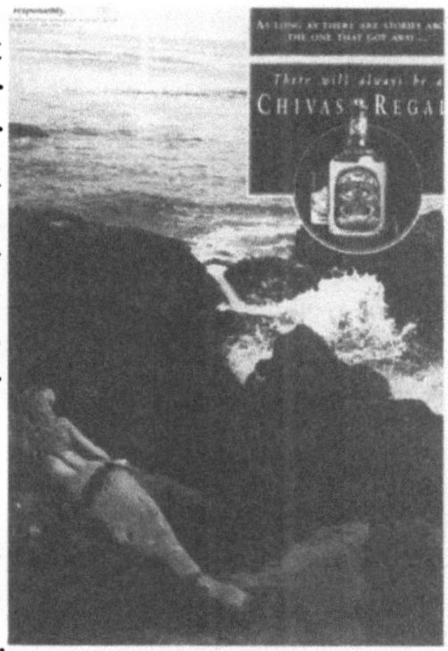

4.15 CHIVAS REGAL: Whiskey

As sex sells perfumes, cars, and clothes, so it also sells whiskey. The CHIVAS advertisement elevates a common fishing fib to the realm of myth. While no one admittedly believes in sea nymphs or mermaids, everyone is attracted to the possibility. If this brand of Scotch whiskey can open the door to that idea, it will endure long popularity: thus there will always be a CHIVAS REGAL.

HENNESSY COGNAC has "wrapped" its campaign in sensual words that offer an interesting and unique combination: taste and feel: "If you've ever been wrapped in silk*you* already know the feeling of Cognac Hennessy."[38] The visuals are also striking. We notice several things: 1) The advertisement is directed toward women. Most liquor ads are directed towards men, or to men and women sharing a

[37] The "mermaid," it might be argued, is not exactly a "classical" creation. The half-human/half-fish of Greek art are usually males, Tritons or "mermen." But sea-nymphs abound in ancient legend, while the most famous of representations of Amphitrite, bride of Poseidon, shows her as a mermaid—see the their wedding in fresco from Piazza Amerina.

[38] Hennessy's "wrapped" advertisements were published widely in 1994; one example appeared in *Playboy* (February, 1994).

drink together; in the Cognac Hennessy ad, no man is visible; 2) Still the ad is sexually evocative; the woman is portrayed so as to be desirable to a man: as he reaches for the cognac he reaches for her. The Hennessy woman seems to be in a transported state, apparently from tasting the Cognac, but the image is ambiguous: maybe she is transported by the silk; 3) The cognac itself is shown in glasses from above, so the images appear almost as lenses rather than as liquid; 4) The woman is "wrapped in silk"--but how many women have been?—but part of the silk is in an arch above her: a scarf billowing around her. It is this billowing piece of silk that turns the picture into a classical image, a conceit which also renders the scene erotic, for the arching scarf is part of every ancient portrayal (vase painting, mosaic, fresco) of a sea love story. We see it in the depictions of Zeus & Europa, of Poseidon & Amphitrite, of Aphrodite on her shell; sometimes, indeed, as here, the arching veil is present even when the figures are on land, as in illustrations of the Judgment of Paris, where Aphrodite is so surrounded.

We have here an advertisement that draws inspiration from classical art for its visual appeal: we are assumed to know the erotic implications of the image. The full sensuality of the ad comes from the verbal linking of an external physical sensation and an internal one: taste implies touch, touch defines taste. Cognac Hennessy made the phrase a slogan for a long-lasting campaign, interesting in that it assumes an uncommon experience as a common denominator for those who will drink the liquor.

ADVERTISING & MYTHOLOGY CELEBRATE THE LIBERATED WOMAN

During the 1950s manufactured products were advertised to the woman as homemaker and happy wife. In the 1960s and 1970s, the female shopper was encouraged to buy articles to enhance her appearance so as to attract a male. Then in the late 1980s and 1990s a concentration of advertisements centered upon the liberated woman began to appear. While VIRGINIA SLIMS had long celebrated women's emancipation from male stereotype, the ads of the 90s celebrated the woman who had found herself as a woman. NIKE, for example ran several page advertisements for the woman who ran alone. The text began: "You are not a goddess..." but the suggestion was that the new woman was indeed close to divinity, that the female athlete was nearly a modern deity. NIKE created mini-stories for the woman who would run in its shoes, stories which celebrated the wearer for striding out alone, for saying yes to life, asserting her closeness to nature and herself.[39] NIKE even created mini-dramas for its shoes. In the October issue of *Cosmopolitan*, for example, NIKE offered "Falling in Love in Six Acts. A Passion Play." In ten pages of illustration and text, the shoe company developed the six steps of a love affair: Lust, Euphoria, Fear, Disgust, The Truth, and The Finale, accompanying each description with an illustration (or two) of a woman in some athletic pursuit. Through its advertisements NIKE intended to do more than sell shoes or even a life style, although the latter was certainly part of its aim. The company wished to create a literature, a cultural artifact, and finally, a new mythology, of which a woman (or a man, for similar stories were created for men's magazines) could be come a part by purchasing a pair of NIKE shoes.

Other companies also chose to suggest woman's power in a world she now controlled. Women attired in new fabrics appeared backlit by a burst of lightning, the usual weapon of Zeus, and, as we shall see in Chapter V, women replaced Atlas in holding aloft various substitute worlds.

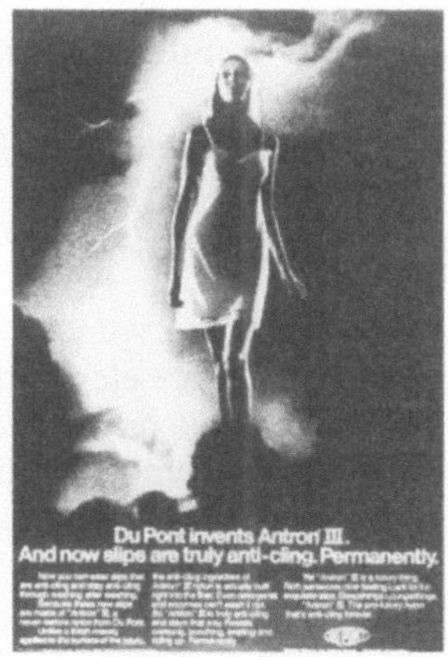

4.16 Du Pont: *Antron* Slip

The identification of the modern woman with the earliest and greatest of the ancient goddesses, Mother Earth, became a popular trope. Indeed, in the late 1980s and 1990s, a new cult for the Earth Mother arose and was practiced in certain parts of California, while the destructive weather of the mid-1990s prompted many to believe in the vengeance of Mother Nature, a term currently in use but clearly referring to the Earth Goddess.

Thus for women's magazines in the summer of 1994, the Coca-Cola Company produced as its advertisement for diet Sprite an illustration and text that recalled the power of the great earth-mother goddess, known in Greek myth as Gaea or Ge.[40] Painted in various shades of green the ad presented a woman, the

---

[39] The NIKE advertising campaign for women was developed in 1990 by Janet Champ and Charlotte Moore, working at the Wieden & Kennedy ad agency, the company which took over the Nike account in 1982. Champ realized that women do not respond to sports heroes as men do, but prefer ads that suggest ordinary women can achieve their individual goals. Information from Eva Pomica, "They Just Did It," (*Lears*, March/1993): 129-130.

[40] The ad appeared widely in 1994, including *Cosmopolitan* (July, 1994).

globe of earth and a radiant sky. The woman, dressed in a flowing green dress and a short green velvet jacket, stands atop the green earth's orb, holding aloft to the green ray-streaked sky a can of diet Sprite. The text, filling the page except for the square of the illustration and the picture of a glass of Sprite next to the can, asserts (in green ink):

> You're a woman of the 90's. Bold, self-assured and empowered. Climbing the ladder of success at work and the StairMaster™ at the gym. You're socially aware and politically correct. But you probably know **all** this already because every ad and magazine has told you a zillion times.
>
> **NO wonder you're thirsty.**
>
> Beneath the glass of diet Sprite and its can is further text and trademark:
>
> Cool, Crisp, Clear. Obey Your Thirst.™

While the woman on top of the world is to be considered an image of success, there are elements to the advertisement that suggest the advertisement is intended to give its product mythic status. The prevailing green color is the most immediate indicator that the woman has greater stature: she is closely associated with the earth on which she stands, i.e., she is an earth goddess, not merely a successful woman of the workplace. Her attire itself is also a clue she is not a business woman, for it is not a power costume but an alluring one, her empowerment comes from her gender not her commercial achievement. More curious is the relationship between text and picture. Why should being "socially aware and politically correct" result in thirst? While both climbing the ladder of success and the StairMaster might arouse it, neither action appears in the illustration.

But classical myth offers an answer. Gaea/Ge as earth goddess was indeed thirsty and was thought to be satisfied by the rain of the sky-god Ouranos [Uranus]. Sprite's green female is boldly facing a cloudy green sky from which golden-green rays fall upon her; it is not at all clear whether these are warmth from the sun or showers from a storm. This successful woman is enjoined to obey [her] thirst. It could be a thirst for success, it could be a thirst to be satisfied within the old ritual of the *hieros gamos*, the "holy marriage" between heaven and earth. Through the careful manipulation of traditional mythic symbols, the Coca-Cola company has created an advertisement appropriate for the 1990s that draws from the earliest legends of western culture.

The female in calm control was a popular image in advertisements of 1993-1994. Whether she was the huntress of TAGHeuer watches (see below), a power to disturb the equilibrium for *Catalyst* perfume, or the successful athlete portrayed in NIKE stories, she was a frequent subject of Madison Avenue's attention. Thus she became the subject of the advertisements for H.I.S. Jeans.

In the winter and spring of 1994 H.I.S. offered an intriguing illustration to promote its jeans for women.[41] The very name of Henry I. Siegel's attire arouses interest: clothes for women called H.I.S. The advertisement in question ran with the caption "H.I.S. DREAM. H.I.S. JEANS." We are uncertain as to whether the woman wearing them is the subject of male fantasy or her own desire. The illustration is equally ambiguous. An old model white jaguar is parked in an Arcadian landscape. A canoe is carefully fastened on top, its paddler rests against the trunk. Beside the car, facing us, stands a woman in a tight-fitting halter-top black evening dress; she has on long black gloves and a diamond bracelet adorns her wrist. She stands tensely erect, holding two long fishing poles. Her stance suggests at first glance that the poles are rather a large bow and her scarf a quiver; we are compelled to look at her more closely. Floating in the top right of the picture is a pair of jeans. Under the picture we read "Jeans that fit your life."

Nothing about the illustration itself tells us this is an advertisement for women's sports attire. But it does recall ancient mythology. The landscape, reminiscent of the rugged wilds of Arcadia, and the woman's fearful calm stare immediately bring to mind Artemis, Greek goddess of the hunt. The patron deity of hunters, protector of young animals, and bringer of death to women was known to haunt the mountains of central Greece, the land knownto this day as the province of Arcadia. There she would initiate swift and relentless punishment of any who angered her, and her anger was easily aroused. The young hunter Actaeon innocently came into the clearing where the deity and her band of nymphs were bathing in a mountain stream. Even as he staggered back and turned away, Artemis initiated his doom: transformed into a stag, he was hunted down and torn apart by his own hounds.

The woman in the H.I.S. advertisement recalls such controlled and deadly power. The life that these jeans fit must be one where women dominate. If she is the

---

[41] The advertisement appeared in *Playboy* (January, 1994) and similar magazines.

subject of male fantasy, it is one that must be carefully dreamed. If, on the other hand, the wearer of H.I.S. jeans gains this power by so dressing, the popular article of attire must be purchased and worn with very deliberate intent by a very special type of woman. By donning H.I.S. jeans, a woman gains wide-reaching control.

Artemis' power in the 1990s was not limited to H.I.S. jeans advertisements. The motto for the Swiss made TAGHeuer watch is "Don't Crack Under Pressure." This theme is illustrated with various images of models, male and female, in situations of sport and its stress. In the summer of 1994 TAGHeuer's model was a woman taking careful aim with bow and arrow.[42] Interpreted in terms of mythology the action, pose and attitude recalled the goddess Artemis.

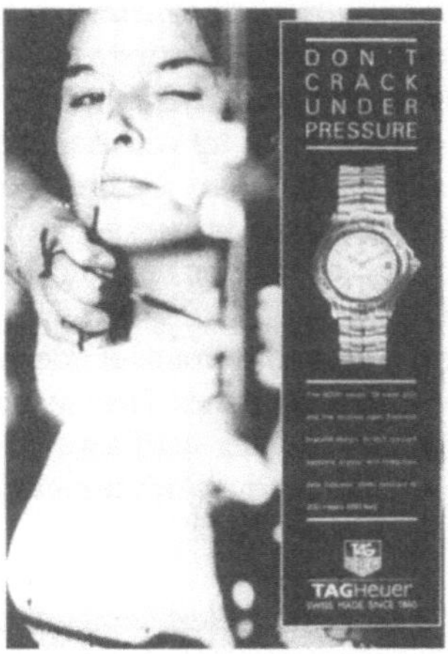

4.17 TAGHeuer. Watch

The Greek goddess of the hunt- although also the protectress of young animals- was relentless in her pursuit of both game and those who offended her. The virgin deity was easily angered; her mythology records the ruin she wrought upon those who crossed her path even innocently. Her weapon was the bow and arrow, and with these she not only hunted her prey, both human and beast, but also brought death to women.

The multiplicity and ambiguity of her spheres of power and influence resulted from the syncretism of her assimilation into Greek cult. Brought from the East, where she was originally a fertility goddess, as her many-breasted statue at her wondrous temple at Ephesus showed, she became in Greece a deity associated with Selene, goddess of the moon and hence in care of women and their natural functions. As sister of Apollo she was considered to share some of his functions: as he brought disease and death to men, she ended the life of women. But whereas Apollo became more and more closely associated with art and the refinements of civilization, worshiped at his fixed temple at Delphi, Artemis remained in the wilds of Arcadia, devoting herself to the care of young animals and aiding the virtuous hunter.

The TAGHeuer archer exemplifies the calm control of this expert huntress. Her steady eye recalls determined purpose: a wrong doer will pay- there is no room

42. The advertisement was in all magazines, including *Esquire* (June, 1994).

for pity or forgiveness. The wearer of this Swiss watch will be in total control and need fear no opposition.[43]

In the fall of 1995, magazines suddenly featured a new type of advertisement: an ad for one product which also advertised another. IBM promoted its ThinkPad®701C in use by Gianni Versace for his "boldly creative designs."[44] It is on his IBM ThinkPad that the fashion designer develops his ideas. A new mythological theme also enters the advertising world with this promotion.

The IBM illustration is of a lavish bedroom adorned with various classical statues: an Apollo Belvedere stands at the right, a soft sunlight filters in through the open window behind him, a Theseus, an Aphrodite and an Artemis are also present, as well as a bronze Etruscan figurine fashioned into a candelabra. The presence of such figures is not new, although to support the latest in computers with ancient Greek statues is a rather unusual conceit. Centered is the IBM ThinkPad®701C, with a sleek sailboat in a rockbound harbor on its screen, but this image is not unique.

What is new in this art-within-art advertisement is the picture which hangs over Gianni Versace's big bed, a bed surrounded and littered with various other objects of opulence. The circular painting, a copy of Claude-François Vignon's neoclassical interpretation of the Choice of Heracles (now in the Louvre), is an interesting selection. The advertisement's text serves to unite image and idea:

> Working from the bedroom of his Lake Como villa Versace draws on neoclassical surroundings for design inspiration, using his ThinkPad to freely experiment with color and style. An approach that, uniquely, marries 18th century art with 20th-century technology.

---

[43] In the May, 1994 advertisements for the watch, a similar huntress is portrayed. Here she is not an archer but rather a horse rider and hence need not be considered in this mythological study. Ancient Amazons were women warriors who rode horses, but hatless and bare breasted. TagHeuer's female in these advertisements is ready for the hunt dressed in British style.

[44] The advertisement appeared everywhere, including *Travel & Leisure* (October, 1995).

The painting depicts the moment when the mighty hero must choose between a life of virtue or one of vice.[45] The two temptations are portrayed as women. Vice is shown as a Venus attended by several Cupids, one of whom leans against a Herm of Dionysus, while the woman's dress is slipping down in the usual manner of the love-goddess' robe. Virtue is depicted as a woman demurely attired and holding a writing tablet on her lap. A naked youth stands behind her; he seems to be effortlessly withstanding a serpent's attack. As Virtue's path is supposed to be attended by hardship, this figure may represent potential struggles. In the center of the painting stands Heracles, nude, identified by his customary attribute, the mighty club. He looks toward Vice who extends her arms to him, indeed has grasped his unyielding arm. But immediately beside him stands Athena, attired in a brilliant blue robe and her towering bronze helmet. She, too, looks toward Vice, but gestures in the other direction. The hero is tempted, but he will follow the Goddess of Wisdom.

Gianni Versace's creations, as we have seen, seem to draw more inspiration from the gods of passion than those of wisdom and restraint; perhaps Herakles' choice served as a guiding light for Versace, an inspiration to keep him turned to requisite reason. The IBM advertisement leaves these questions for the viewer to consider. The ad's immediate intent is to show how the ancient world can be brought to bear upon the modern by the use of its contemporary technology. In this way IBM has offered a new insight into the role of classical mythology in modern advertising.

---

[45] The parable was told by Prodicus of Ceos, and is quoted by both Xenophon (*Memorabilia* 2.21-34) and Cicero (*De Officiis* I.118).

V
THE CLASSICAL CONCEIT

Equally intriguing are those advertisements that play with a classical conceit. Sometimes the expected is reversed, the traditional is altered, and knowledge of the original is necessary to understand the new message. Sometimes the new interpretation gains from the novelty and is thus successful, at other times the alteration obscures the message, leaving ambiguity in place of clarity. With the ambiguous advertisement as with the altered one, the audience must know the myth that inspired the image.

ALTERED STATES

One of the most popular figures with which to play in advertisements is Atlas. The Titan who chose to stand against Zeus in the Battle between Titans and Olympians was condemned by the victorious Zeus to stand at the edge of the universe and support its weight on his shoulders. Only once did he get to lay it aside: when Heracles volunteered to hold the world while Atlas fetched him the golden apples from the Garden of the Hesperides. Upon his return, Atlas showed no more wisdom than when he had opted for the Titan cause, for when Heracles asked him to take back the world while he fetched a pillow, the Titan shouldered his burden once more. Heracles, of course, took the apples and brought them to Mycenae, leaving Atlas to his destiny.

Numerous representations of Atlas supporting the world appear in post-classical statuary. Indeed, it was because an illustration of the Titan at his post adorned the front cover of Mercator's 16th century collection of maps that all future map collections bear his name.

Numerous advertisements of men supporting a globe on their shoulders, or raising it above their head appear in print media. In all examples, the idea of punishment is gone: Atlas' strength is celebrated. In the 1990s, a new trend developed: the woman as Atlas. In a world of sex equality, the female has the strength of the male. Again and again we, the viewing public, are shown a woman supporting a great sphere on her outstretched arms. In most instances another image could have offered the same message, but the ad creators have selected Atlas-as-woman to promote the product or event.

One such use of the symbol is that created by Vidal Sassoon as the poster/ad for the Vidal Sassoon Academy's Long Beach International Beauty Expo, an illustration appearing in magazines during the summer and fall of 1995.[1] Here in a shapely drawing an unclad woman stands on her toes and holds the world above her head; her beautifully groomed hair flows down her back. Wavy lines form a deep valley rising steeply on either side of the drawing as a background for woman and globe. These wavy bands resemble either flowing locks of hair- the most logical association for Vidal Sassoon- or the streams of the ocean which in traditional Greek myth surrounded the disk of the earth, upon which earth's land mass floated. Brilliant colors enhance the poster/ad, and although no further information about the event is given (date, time, even place in Long Beach is not printed), the striking image makes sure that the viewer is aware of the Vidal Sassoon Academy and its international exposition and thus will, perhaps, seek how to become part of it. The simple drawing is intended to promote "the benefits of a high education" for one's hair. Other images might have served to carry the same message; the choice of Atlas as the mythic paradigm underscores two ideas: the strength of (the beautiful) woman and the value of a higher education so that one understands the Atlas allusion. Woman, according to this advertisement, holds the world in her hands, and the woman who uses Vidal Sassoon Hair Care System™ may find herself endowed with Titanic powers.

The most subtle of the mid-1990s Atlas advertisements was that of Coty's *Nokomis* ("the fragrance that speaks to a woman's soul").[2] Next to a text "Woman. Creative, intuitive, mystical and magical," stands a woman in a back-plunging black gown gently supporting a golden orb of uncertain material. A golden sunset fills the page. Her creative...magical nature, empowered by Coty's fragrance, gives her the ability to emulate Atlas; it is on her shoulders the world rests. Unlike the Titan, however, the *Nokomis* woman holds up her globe effortlessly.

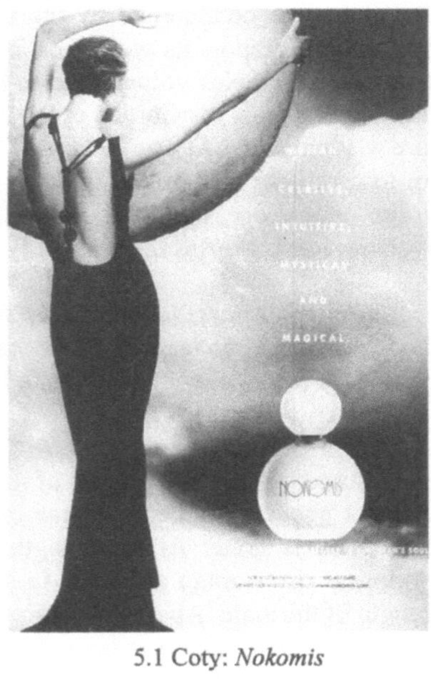

5.1 Coty: *Nokomis*

[1] Again, the advertisement was ubiquitous, including *Glamour* (September, 1995).

[2] The advertisement appeared widely in 1997, including in *Red Book* (July: 1997).

We saw in Chapter III how PERRY ELLIS in the early 1990s offered for its *360°* perfume a variation on the Zeus and Europa story, where the myth's parts are all there--woman, bovine, sea-- but altered, the image reversed. In 1995 Perry Ellis returned to classical myth and offered an illustration remarkably evocative of the story of Hades' abduction of Persephone.[3] According to the Greek legend, Demeter's daughter attracted the attention of the ruler of the realm of the dead. Hades caused a brilliant flower to spring up in front of the young girl, and as she reached for it, he sprang from a rocky cave and carried her off. Demeter searched the world in vain for her lost child, and let the earth go fallow during her quest. Finally the gods of Olympus told her the truth and tried to persuade Hades to return the girl. He refused. Then Zeus brokered an arrangement: Persephone could be with her mother for two thirds of the year, but must return to the realm of the dead for the final third.[4] Thus did the Greeks explain the changing seasons; Persephone was with her mother in the spring and summer, with Hades during the winter months. The whole story of Demeter's search and the possibility of rebirth formed the beliefs and ritual of the Greek's most important religious festival, those of the Mysteries celebrated at Eleusis late every summer.

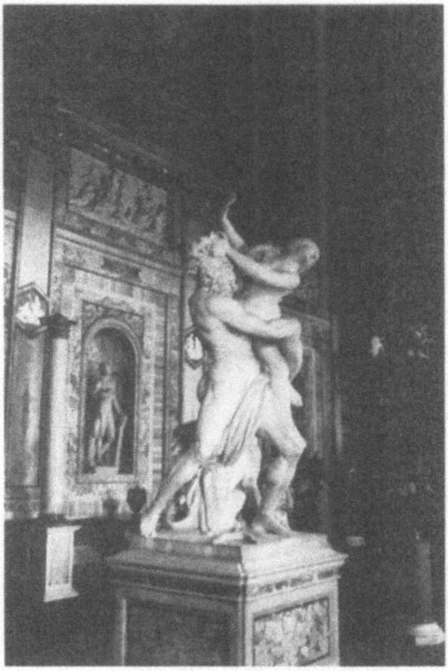

5.2 Hades & Persephone. Bernini. Rome \ Galleria Borghese

Paintings in various media from the classical and medieval period portrayed Hades' abduction of the girl. Since the Renaissance Bernini's sculpture of the event has defined the image. Any other sculpture or drawing which portrays or alludes to the story looks to his statue group for inspiration. And it is the idea, I suggest, that informs Perry Ellis' 1995

[3] The ad appeared in all the usual women's magazines and in *People* (September, 1995).

[4] Persephone had eaten some seeds of a pomegranate while with Hades; one who has eaten in the Realm of the Dead must remain there. Zeus' arrangement returned the girl to the light.

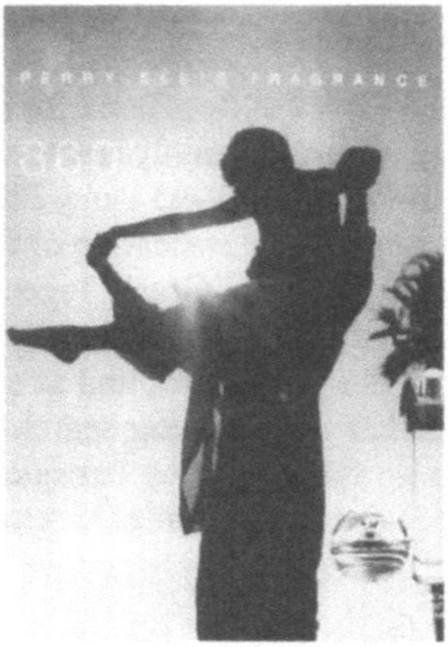

5.3 Perry Ellis: *360°*

advertisement for his *360°* perfume. Seen almost entirely in silhouette is a man carrying aloft a young woman; he is clothed in black, her grey veils flow down around him. Light emanating from behind the figures heightens the dark color and the statuesque quality of the figures recall Bernini's famous sculpture. The intent of the ad is surely to suggest that the*360°* perfume transports its wearer and this picture shows a moment of joy. But like the earlier Perry Ellis advertisement, ambiguity shadows the illustration, for Bernini's sculpture records a moment of violence and fear. The woman who wears *360°* will find her life changed, turned about and filled with excitement. But these aspects are won only with some risk. The advertisement, intended to portray a time of new romance, compels the informed viewer to consider that there may be a second and deeper implication.

While the *360°* advertisement made a subtle allusion to the rape of Persephone, the story had been recalled openly and dramatically in an advertisement for Tollana. Champagne appearing in wine magazines some ten years earlier.[5] Here the traditional representation of Hades springing up from his rocky cave and carrying off a frightened Persephone is graphically portrayed, accompanied by a text that puns upon the dry quality of the Australian champagne: the BRUT from DOWN UNDER. It is an arresting advertisement, suggesting the rough excitement of life at the southern edge of the

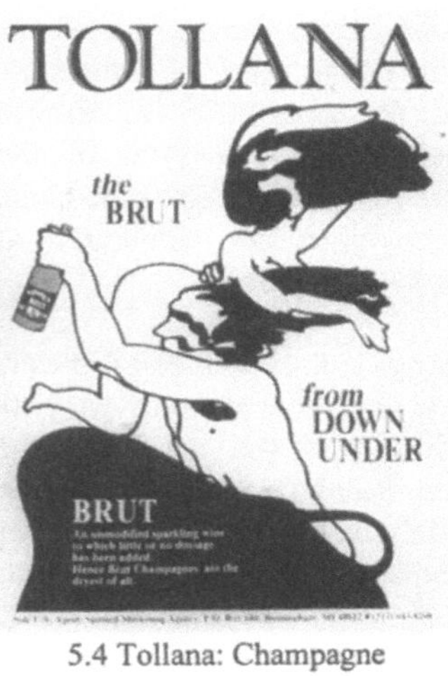

5.4 Tollana: Champagne

[5] This advertisement appeared in the *Friends of Wine* magazine in December, 1984.

world. It manages to be both humorous and learned (the reader must know the myth and its artwork). But the message for Tollana's champagne remains ambiguous, for Hades' abduction of Persephone must imply some danger for the woman who drinks this wine.

A similarly ambiguous message comes from a spring, 1995, advertisement for RALPH LOREN'S *Safari*.[6] Here we see a man holding a tiger cub in his arms, while a woman stands behind him, resting against his shoulder. The man and the tiger imply a certain Dionysian element. In Greek legend and society, as portrayed, for instance, by Euripides in his *The Bacchae*, men, women and nature could act in harmony when celebrating Dionysus. When threatened, however, even women would become violent, rending live animals and turning staves to spears. The line between mortal and beast was thin and easily crossed; the follower of Dionysus was often portrayed (as suggested elsewhere) as out of control, caught in wild emotion, but there was a further aspect to the practice of the cult. As Euripides' play so clearly shows, the interaction of humans and nature can create a community of blissful harmony or wanton destruction. Dionysus is a god whose rites are followed at some risk.

As there is no text with RALPH LOREN'S *Safari* advertisement, we are asked to create our own story for it, but the apparent bond between man, woman and tiger brings the Dionysian cult most quickly to mind. We are also left to wonder what scent we are supposed to capture: that of man the hunter or that of the wild beast? And which one is the girl after?

Another 1990s cologne for men sports a misplaced myth in its name rather than in the scent's promotional copy. The creator of the new aroma wanted to suggest the possibility of both heroic action and mysterious quest: what better myth than that of Theseus and the Minotaur? Theseus, prince of Athens, volunteered to liberate his city from its obligation to send seven youths and seven maidens each year to Crete in expiation for an act of violence against an ambassador from the island kingdom. Those who went there were forced into competition with the Minotaur, a half man, half bull creature who was kept at the center of the labyrinth at Knossos. This monster was the result of the crazed and illicit union of Pasiphaë, queen of Crete and wife of Minos, and a bull to which Aphrodite made her attracted. Minos has Daedalus construct the labyrinth to hide the result of his wife's wanton act. Theseus, at the head of the tribute band, enlisted the aid of Ariadne, princess of Crete; at her suggestion he trailed a string behind him as he approached

---

[6] The advertisement appeared, e.g., in *Gourmet* (May, 1995)

the hidden monster, and having successfully slain the beast he retraced Ariadne's twine to the daylight.

A few facts of history seem to underlie this story. Since the discovery of Knossos by Sir Arthus Evans in the early 1900s, the existence of a labyrinthine palace has been known, while frescoes found within its ruins portray the Minoan sport of bull-jumping: grabbing the horns of a bull and vaulting in a somersault over its back. Furthermore, it is known that around 1400 B.C., the people of mainland Greece, the Mycenaean Greeks, conquered the Minoans on the island of Crete. It was an easy step for the Athenians to claim that their hero was responsible for the conquest of the Minotaur and, by implication, the conquest of the Minoans.

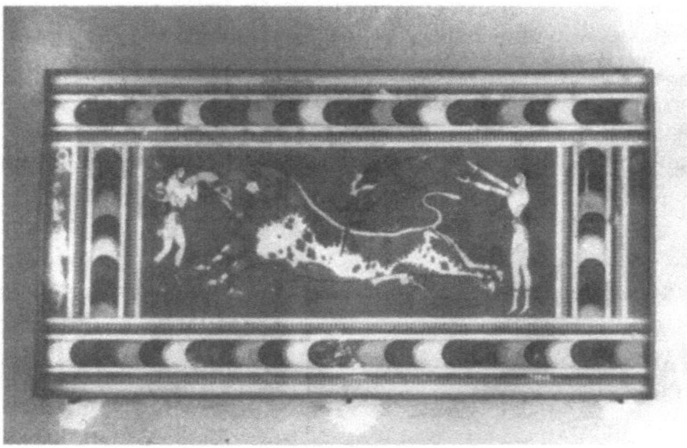

5.5 "Bull Jumping" Fresco. Crete \ Palace of Knossos

The story of Theseus and the Minotaur was popular with ancient artists in all media, while Picasso also painted a famous and (typically) ambiguous illustration of the legend, as well as several drawings more directly based on ancient vase paintings. Thus when Paloma Picasso came out with her new scent for men, her choice of name seemed doubly appropriate: *Minotaure*. During the last several years, the advertisements for Paloma Picasso's new scent were ubiquitous and hence the public had ample opportunity to consider its potential.[7] In the initial promotional campaign, we saw the hero at the entrance to the labyrinth; a ring in the Greek meander design gleamed on his finger. Turned away from us, he peers boldly into the stone walls of the Minoan palace. The Minotaur, object of his quest, is imagined to be just out of view (it is interesting that the mythological beast is not shown; the

[7]The advertisement appeared in many magazines, sample "sniff sheets" were handed out in shopping malls as late as 1996. One of the earliest ads was in *Playboy* (January, 1994).

advertisement's creator assumes we know the story). Courage and mystery combine. But--just what are we to imagine the cologne smells like? The sweating fear of Theseus or the aroma of the man-beast? While, actually, the scent is quite pleasant and surely popular, its name remains highly suspect.

5.6 Paloma Picasso: *Minotaure*

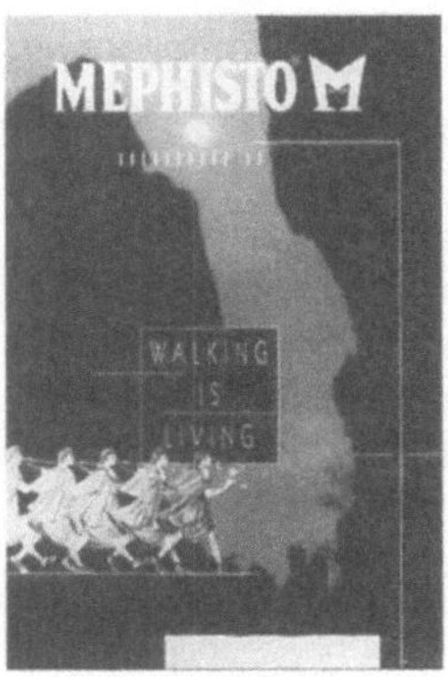

5.7 Mephisto: Shoes

Mythic ambiguity in ads was not limited to the olfactory realm, to fragrances for both sexes. Shoes for men and women by MEPHISTO, with the slogan "Original MEPHISTO. Copies are but copies", burst upon the American scene in the fall of1995. The advertisements featured large pull-out sections in which the German company displayed numerous examples of their acclaimed walking shoes, a series of models still said to be "just a small selection from the international Mephisto collection." [8] The first page of the advertisement, however, does not feature any individual pair of shoes. It displays a process-sion of six men in classical attire, each playing a Greek double flute (aulos) as he strides enthusiastically along. But the walkers are not wearing ancient sandals: modern shoes adorn their feet. A single line of text is printed in the center: "WALKING IS LIVING."

[8] The tear-out advertisements appeared in numerous magazines throughout the fall of 1995, including *Glamour* and *Men's Health.*

The procession of striding figures is given no particular identification, leaving the viewer to create meaning through association with something familiar. The way the walkers are portrayed, like the figures on ancient vases, the classic costume, the ancient flute, suggest this is a special moment, a moment in a significant ritual. A procession is part of many religious ceremonies, either when the celebrants advance to the sacred area, to a place of special pilgrimage, or when the holy icon is carried around its building. With the promotional phrase, "walking is living," we are offered a clue as to which sacred procession the advertisement should bring to mind.

The central day of the Eleusinian Mysteries' celebration was the day of the *pompe*, the procession, when all initiates and their guides walked the 14 miles from Athens to Eleusis. It was a day of joyous parade, joyous perhaps from the very procession itself, but also for the promise that the Eleusinian cult held: a better life now and in the future. This cult offered its followers a form of worship wherein the focus lay on the individual and how he/she could improve her/his life: a personal religion as opposed to that of the state. The illustration in the MEPHISTO advertisement recalls that procession of initiates on the *pompe* day of the festival. This ritual is portrayed, for instance, on a stele fragment and on the Niniion tablet, both now in the museum at Eleusis. The clue to the promotion for MEPHISTO shoes lies, perhaps, in its similarity to the joyous Eleusinian procession.

One of the more bizarre advertisements to appear in print media in 1994 was that offered by KRIZIA. In a photograph by Helmut Newton we see a model who, although her facial expression is calm would seem to be in rather dire straits.[9] She is pinned by the sleeves of her KRIZIA sweater dress to an isolated cliff by the edge of the sea. As her feet, protected in high-heeled boots, rest upon the rocks at sea level, perhaps her calm visage indicates she is asleep, that she is in no danger of falling to her death in the sea below. But we cannot be sure.

This advertisement appeared frequently in several women's magazines so it was clearly supposed to carry a positive message. What that message means, however, is not immediately evident. The dress is able to be stretched without tearing? But no woman needs to extend her sleeves three or more feet beyond her wrists. While the model is not, finally, suspended by her sleeves, she is not in a comfortable or even enticing situation, pinned thus against a rough rock with the waves lapping at her feet. With her upper thighs exposed, she must suffer from cold as well as the discomfort of the rock.

[9] Among other places, the advertisement appeared in *Mademoiselle* (June, 1994).

We noted in Chapter III that Helmut Newton liked to offer an allusion to a classical myth in his advertising photographs. Here again the design of the KRIZIA advertisement recalls an ancient legend. As in the Leda and the swan illustration, the mythic reference is wrapped in ambiguity, and only those who know the whole story would choose to purchase this dress. A woman stranded, exposed, on a sea cliff recalls the story of Andromeda. This princess was put out on a rocky tor by her father, acting in response to a punishing command of the gods. There on the sea-girt promontory the maiden was at the mercy of nature and a particularly rough sea monster. However, Andromeda was soon rescued by Perseus, who came winging by her cliff on his return from slaying the gorgon Medusa. He carried the princess off to his home island of Seriphos, where they married and lived happily for many years. In time Perseus returned to his ancestral home in Argos to compete in some athletic contests, where his discus toss went wild and accidently killed his grandfather Acrisius.[10] Thus exiled from Argos, Perseus and Andromeda, according to some versions of the legend, then founded the citadel of Mycenae. Newton's picture for the 1994 KRIZIA advertisement is eye catching, but its message rests in ancient mythology. The woman who recognizes the story of Andromeda and her rescue by Perseus in this ad is the one who will select this knit dress.

Myth and the classical world can be the basis for humorous advertisements as well. An interesting series of ads for the 1997 Mercury Tracer appeared in 1996.[11] In a cartoon strip, under the heading "As Seen On Radio" a young man announces that he is "strapped to the top of this Tracer here at the Parthenon in Greece....while our driver is listening to 'Zorba The Greek' on the 6-CD stereo." The Tracer is then pictured driving down the "537 steps" with the bumps smoothed out by the car's suspension--which can then easily smooth out "more timeless things...like potholes." "537 steps"? At no time did Athena's temple have 537 steps. The temple, like other Doric temples, stood on a 3-step base, while there were no more than a dozen steps at the Periclean entry court. Nor are there that many steps to the acropolis itself. But while the Tracer advertisement failed on accuracy, the allusion certainly attracted attention- if the number of my students who brought me a copy of it is any indication! So while the purist might hesitate to purchase a Tracer (would it be manufactured with any more attention to detail?), the humor of the advertisement might well jog others into considering it, for the parody of the classical gives the Mercury auto the same cachet as the Venus di Milo gave the MAZDA.

---

[10] By this action Perseus fulfilled the prophecy which had foretold that he would slay Acrisius, father of Danaë, Perseus' unhappy mother. Her story is told in Chapter III.

[11] The advertisement appeared in most magazines, including *Live* (July, 1996).

Thus the influence of the ancient world, even when imperfectly remembered and employed, or deliberately parodied, remains powerful. Each of these advertisements carries a message that must be understood in terms of classical myth. The association with Greek and Roman ideas adds a deeper dimension to the advertisement. Even when the myth underscores the wrong image or offers an uncertain message, the advertisement still has value. For the addition of the Muse makes us remember it, and in remembering the ad we are closer to purchasing the product.

VI
THE COMPANY LOGO.

Mythological figures continue to live as brand logos. A goodly number of companies have adopted ancient deities and creatures as logos to promote their name or brand. There is a repetition of images, not surprising if we consider the rather limited range of viable options, but noteworthy is the unusual choice of mythological figures, the subtle ways images have been translated to offer new meanings. In a fine study titled *Mythmaking on Madison Avenue*, Sal Randazzo asserts, "The Greeks had their pantheon of gods; Americans have brands."[1] Randazzo's concern is to show "how advertisers apply the power of myth to create leadership brands."

As everything we use has a brand name (excluding those few that use the term "generic"), we are constantly reminded of product's trade name. A trade or brand name has been chosen or manufactured for one major purpose: to advertise that product as made by that company. A company devotes much time, effort, and legal research in choosing a name for its product.[2] The name must persuade the buyer to distinguish between item A and item B: the shopper must reach for Ajax™ or Comet™ cleanser, must select Imperial™ or Blue Bonnet™ margarine.

Trade names also are often derived from ancient mythology. The deities and heroes of Greece and Rome add instant class to a product. These familiar names are easier, in a way, than names associated with actual history or invented names. The former can be limited by time or place (although some real live persons have acquired a mythic aura, Pochohantas or Davy Crockett, for example). An invented name must be checked carefully to see that it does not replicate or reflect similar names, it must be appropriate and pronounceable in languages of all countries where it is to be marketed (the "infamous" example of the Chevy NOVA in Mexico, for instance, where *no va* means "it doesn't go"), it must have favorable connotations and, if possible, be visually comprehensive and easily illustrated. If name and logo can be linked, that is especially good, as in the case of NIKE (see below), but a logo can go a long way in adding status and making a company's name memorable. In this chapter I

---

[1] Sal Randazzo, *Mythmaking on Madison Avenue. How Advertisers Apply the Power of Myth and Symbolism to Create Leadership Brands*. (Chicago: Probus, 1993):49.

[2] For a discussion of these considerations, see Adrian Room, *Dictionary of Trade Name Origins* (London: 1982): 1-18. Room's examples are those on the British market, but his points apply to the trade name issues of any nation.

identify the mythological images some companies have chosen as their logos and used to attract attention.[3]

Some names and images are rather obvious choices: Dionysus or Bacchus, who gave wine to mortals, naturally serves to promote various wines and liquors; Gaea, Mother Earth, graces a vial of Herbal Essence™ shampoo; Prometheus promotes Kingsford Match Light™, as he fought Zeus himself to give fire to mortals; Demeter/Ceres, goddess of grain, protects Gold Medal™ flour. It is even appropriate for Ajax, the bravest of the heroes to fight at Troy, to represent a strong cleanser. A nice transfer of image occurs when Athena promotes White Owl™ cigars, for her special bird was the owl; her owl was engraved on the coins of Athens.

The penetration of myth into condom names is one of the more intriguing aspects of this theme; ancient legend has entered popular culture through prophylactics. In the designated area of drug and other stores labels sport such names as Trojan, Spartan, or Mentor. Clearly the choice of name for Trojan or Spartan was to suggest strength and valor: the warriors of Troy protected their city for 10 long years, while the Spartan soldier was known for his commitment to battle; he was to come home with his shield or on it. Of course, the Trojans finally lost, as did the Spartans; one also wonders if it is proper to consider a condom as used in a battlefield situation. One the other hand, the Carter-Wallace name choice is more appealing. In Homer's *Odyssey,* Mentor was the guide and teacher for Telemachus and his name has become synonymous with one who plays that role. Carter-Wallace created its Mentor™ condoms with "a safety seal for even safer sex," and its advertisements give several paragraphs of advice. The trademark phrase, however, is the indication of its name: "The intelligent choice is Mentor." The user of this condom is not a warrior but a thinking man.

These examples are all images taken deliberately from the Greek world. Once in a while a Greek image is chosen completely on whim; the fine book company

---

[3] The companies included here were both prompt and generous in their response to my interest in their logos. I extend them all my deepest gratitude. On the other hand, despite several letters some companies failed to respond to my inquiries as to their choice of logo. Thus some well known company icons are missing here. Adrian Room (note 2 above) reports a similar lack of response from many companies that he contacted; others replied "We regret we cannot give you this information," a response he termed (17) "both tantalizing and infuriating. Did they know but wouldn't tell, or did they themselves not know?"

Daedalus, whose logo is a winged book, was thus christened because its founder, Robin Moody, liked the myth of Daedalus, the inventor, liked Stephen Daedalus in Joyce's *Ulysses,* just liked the name.[4]

Sometimes a picture can obtain mythic status even though not actually based upon any particular legend, an idea graphically portrayed can becomea symbol. Thus, as Stuart and Elizabeth Ewen point out in their interesting work, *Channels of Desire,* the pictures on bags of flour and cans of milk sent to Europe during World War I came to symbolize American values and opportunities and aroused a desire to live in America; it was believed that the country must be the pastoral heaven portrayed on the labels.[5]

Some logos from earlier times have now become collectors' items. For example, from the late 1800s to the 1950s, Florida Citrus growers used colorful paper labels on their wooden crates to attract attention to their product. The vying citrus companies would try to grab the potential buyer not with pictures of their oranges or grapefruits but with alluring women, and some of the brands chose women from classical mythology. The Crescent City Fruit Company, for example, designed a label for its Belle of Crescent City Brand that played off both parts of the name: a lovely lady sits on a smiling crescent moon and offers it an orange. While the images are perfect for the brand name, the idea of Selene the moon-goddess lies behind the design and gives it a certain cachet. There was a double verbal play with this illustration: the crescent moon echoed Crescent City's name, while *Belle* was the alluring female who by name and gender rivaled the women of other citrus labels. By seating her on the moon's horn and showing her feeding its man therein, the company added sexual suggestions to its product. A buyer could easily remember both the name and the possibilities offered by the fruit of this company. Since he was further assured that these oranges were "Seald Sweet" (with 1/4 more juice), there were several good reasons to buy this brand of oranges.

The fruit grown by the McCullough Brothers of Okahumpka was mysteriously given the brand name "Deep Water." The illustration for the name was clear, however:

---

[4] Information from the company, sent to me via e-mail by Alissa Herdershot, customer service representative at Daedalus Books.

[5] Ewen, Stuart and Elizabeth, *Channels of Desire. Mass Images and the Shaping of American Consciousness* (New York et al: McGraw -Hill, 1982): 43-47.

a mermaid/sea nymph twirls a conch shell as waves wash over her and fish swim by her. The graphic is good, although no citrus fruits are in the picture, and the brand name has little to do with the product or its producers. But while there was no viable relationship between the fruit and the ladies of the labels, the idea of attaching divinities to the product remained popular. DEEP WATER relied on the beauty of the mermaid and the excitement of mystery she naturally evokes to arouse the buyer's attention and remain in his memory. These aspects, beauty and excitement, were the qualities the McCullough Brothers hoped to suggest about their citrus products.

Sometimes the choice of a mythological figure as a logo is mysterious. MONTEIL cosmetics, for example, adopted the Sphinx for its logo. A phoenix might suggest rebirth into new beauty, but the Sphinx remains enigmatic.[6] A mysterious creature of myth was given positive promotional qualities when RÉMY MARTIN adopted the Centaur as the logo for its Cognac. In Greek legend, the Centaur, half man, half horse, came into being from the (bizarre!) union of Ixion and a cloud image of Hera, queen of the gods, whom he believed he had seduced. A mortal cannot bed an unwilling divinity, of course, so Zeus substituted a nebulous Hera to Ixion's illicit passion. Ixion was dashed down to Tartarus, the deepest sector of the realm of the dead, where he was tied to an ever-spinning wheel: he became a love-charm because he had tried to charm Hera with love.[7] In due time, the Cloud Hera gave birth to the race of Centaurs. Perhaps as a result of their violent generation, the Greek Centaur was considered a wanton beast. The conflict between Centaurs and various mortals formed the subject of several temple sculptures, the best known of which are the East pediment of the Temple of Zeus at Olympia, where Apollo with a single gesture halts the Centaurs' abduction of Lapith maidens, and those portrayed in the South metopes of the Parthenon on the Athenian acropolis, where man and man-beast struggle for civilization. Only wise Chiron was held to be a gentle teacher, compassionate to the

[6] The origin of the Sphinx seems to have been lost in time. Rick Kinsel, Director of Curatorial Services for Coty, the present owner of Monteil, told me (in correspondence, 10-9-1998) that "because the ownership of Monteil has changed many times, I can offer no insight into how or when the sphinx logo was incorporated." Kinsel was extremely generous in his assistance to my project, as noted above (Chapter IV).

[7] An ancient love-charm was made by tying a bird, the Iynx, to a wheel and spinning it; the rotation was believed to draw, to reel, the beloved to the lover. As Dante will later develop the idea of "sin self-punished is perfect justice" in his *Inferno,* the Greeks created punishments for the great wrong-doers that were appropriate for the deed; thus Tantalus, who committed a culinary crime, was forever tormented with hunger and thirst never satisfied.

sufferings of men. It is gentle aspect of the Centaur that has lived on beyond the classical world, perhaps best portrayed in Botticelli's well-known painting of Athena and the Centaur. Thus today RÉMY MARTIN identifies the Centaur with "power, dynamism, romance and timelessness, characteristics which reflect the brand."[8] But the original choice of the Centaur logo is a far more interesting story.

Emile Rémy Martin, creator of the Champagne Cognac which was to bear his name, lacked a family crest; he needed a symbol, an emblem with power and magic. An avid stargazer, he enjoyed seeking the constellation that marked his date of birth, Sagittarius, whose symbol was the Centaur, half-man, half-horse. After he had investigated the mythology associated with the Centaur, creatures who accompanied Dionysus and the wisest of whom was a physician and the tutor of Achilles and Jason, he realized he had found a perfect symbol. The Centaur was associated in myth with many qualities associated with Cognac, while the mythical beast was also his own special sign. It was his son who drew the design that was to become the Cognac's logo, "who brought the Centaur, first revealed under the stars of Rouillac, to life."[9]

In the company's recent advertising campaign, the Centaur usually shown springing from the M of Martin, now materializes mysteriously in the flame of a cigar, the light glinting from a glass of Cognac, in an ace waiting to be played. The mythical beast brings not only power and romance but also mystery and magic to the one who drinks the fine champagne Cognac.

One of the more audacious creators of apparel and accessories is GIANNI VERSACE. The company's chosen logo is unusual: it is the Gorgon Medusa, the figure from Greek legend with the power to petrify all who fell within her glance, the figure with the apotropaicpower to protect whatever she guarded. The Gorgon's image filled the pediments of many temples: that of Artemis in Corcyra (Corfu), for example, or the early Athena temple on the Acropolis at Athens. VERSACE's was a careful and conscious choice: he wanted his clothes to arrest the buyer's attention, to freeze the shopper in his/her tracks.[10] The designer believed that in the course of time the image

---

[8] Information from Dacotah Sutor, Marketing Assistant for Rémy Martin, in personal correspondence. Ms. Sutor also sent me the pages from Thomas Laurenceau's book. I gratefully acknowledge her assistance.

[9] Information and quotation from Thomas Laurenceau, *RÉMY MARTIN. L'ESPRIT DU COGNAC* (Paris: E.P.A, 1991): 19-22.

[10] That it was indeed this idea which guided the choice of the Medusa (a figure some might

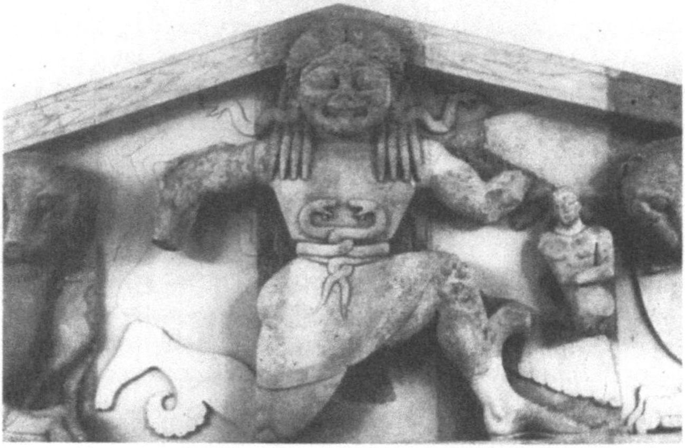

6.1 Gorgon: Corfu \ Artemis Temple

of the Gorgon changed from horrible to alluring, "full of ambiguity and se-duction" like the statue created by Benvenuto Cellini that stands in the Loggia dei Lanzi in Florence or Canova's version placed in the Vatican Museum.[11]

From the blood of the beheaded Medusa the winged horse Pegasus came into being. The story is that when Perseus cut off the gorgon's head, she was pregnant by Poseidon, god of the sea--and of earthquakes, who was also mysteriously associated with horses. The *Homeric Hymn to Poseidon* describes the sea god's various realms thus: "The gods have given to you a double honor, O Earthshaker, to be both a tamer of horses and a savior of ships."[12] In the famous contest with Athena for the patronage of Athens, one version reports that he offered a horse to the Athenians as his gift (other versions say his trident strike magically produced a spring of salt water on the acropolis.) The Athenians preferred the Maiden Goddess' gift of the olive tree. This equine association must lie behind the story of the generation of Pegasus. When the hoof of the winged horse struck the

consider odd or dangerous) was confirmed to me by Donatella Versace in personal correspondence (9-28-1998). She writes, "Therefore he who beholds her (the Gorgon) stands transfixed, seduced by her face."

[11] Donatella Versace referred to the Medusa of Cellini's statue as the inspirational image. My photographs of this statue, however, did not reproduce clearly. Canova's Medusa is equally mysterious, equally seductive.

[12] *Homeric Hymn* 22. We are told the divinity mated even with Demeter in the form of a stallion, a legend that may reflect an earlier understanding of Poseidon as a fertility divinity.

ground of Mt. Helicon, a spring of water gushed forth, Hippocrene, water believed to be the inspiration of the Muses who dwelt on the mountain's slopes.[13]

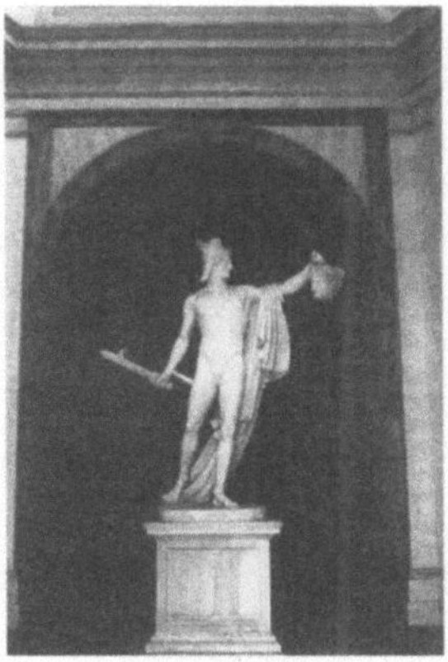

6.2 Perseus. Canova. Rome \ Vatican Museum

Pegasus, then, a magical horse and a source of inspiration, rides high as the symbol of Mobil Oil Company. A predecessor company, Vacuum Oil of South Africa, selected a white Pegasus as a trademark for its gasoline in 1911. In 1924, Standard Oil selected the horse, but in red, when it registered its gasoline in Japan. Vacuum Oil and Standard Oil merged in 1933 and adopted the flying red Pegasus™ as its symbol. Alterations were made in the depiction of the horse in 1955 to allow it to appear on the shield of Mobil; final changes were made in the graphics in 1964. Pegasus remains today as Mobil's primary logo, "associated with speed, power, movement, flight and energy, the spirit of [the] company."[14]

A familiar logo is that of American Express. Printed on every card is a figure in Roman, not Greek, attire. The Roman centurion was chosen as distinctive, sufficiently detailed to be difficult to copy, and to suggest "stability, safety, and security."[15] Since 1958, the Roman Centurion has appeared on all AMEX cards and checks. Here is an example of an image used deliberately, correctly, and effectively.[16]

---

[13] Both Pindar and Euripides enter Pegasus into the legend of Bellerophon, the Corinthian hero who, having mastered the horse with the aid of Athena, went forth on it to fight the Amazons. But he tried to ride his winged horse too high and met his end because he sought to ascend to Mt. Olympus.

[14] Information and quotation sent to me via e-mail by Mark Jacobson, a public relations officer of Mobil Oil Company. I gratefully acknowledge his helpful and prompt response to my inquiry about the Pegasus logo.

[15] The choice is described in a letter from Teresa Park, AMEX, 12-1-1994.

[16] American Express uses its logo for the name of its credit processing subsidiary, calling it the "Centurion Bank."

Equally effective and correctly used is that of GoodYear for its tires. The company chose the winged sandal of Hermes/Mercury to promote its brand in 1900; a story lies behind the choice.[17] On the stairway in the home of Frank A. Seiberling, the founder of the GoodYear Company, stood a statue of this ancient god. Mr. Seiberling thought that the god "embodied many of the characteristics for which GoodYear products were known." When in August of 1900 a board meeting was held to find a suitable trademark for the company, one of the sketches, at Mr. Seiberling's suggestion, was one of the winged foot of Mercury. Everyone present agreed this should be the symbol; it was set in the middle of the company's name (although this original "wingfoot" was larger than the one presently used). Thus was the Wingfoot symbol, "known today in every civilized country on earth" chosen. The company knew its mythology, for the Wingfoot press release continues:

> Mercury in ancient times was the god of trade and commerce; but it was as a swift messenger for all the gods of mythology that he was best known, and as such he has continued to be known through the centuries.

The idea of speed had much to do with GoodYear's selection of the symbol, for the "Wingfooted" Mercury was regarded as a fleet herald of good news. But it is as a herald or carrier of good tidings to users of GoodYear products everywhere that the Wingfoot now stands in the minds of people of the world. The god of travelers will stand guard over the driver using Good Year tires; the buyer who opts for these tires has made the right decision.

Surely the best known Hermes/Mercury logo is the FTD floral messenger. For eighty years the wing-sandaled wing-capped runner has indicated a flower shop that delivers. An internationally recognized logo, the flower-bearing Mercury was originally created in 1936, but the deity himself had appeared as the FTD logo as early as 1914. At that time his image dominated the design, but he still carried his traditional caduceus, albeit adorned with ribbons.[18] The 1936 Mercury bore a box of flowers, but

---

[17] The information comes from the Public Affairs Department of the Goodyear Tire & Rubber Company (no name/ 10-28-1997).

[18] "The Story of the FTD Logo" was sent to me by Erikca Staton and Jane Rubens of FTD Association (FAX correspondence 10-14-1998). The information quoted here comes from the FTD "Story." Prior to 1914, FTD's emblem was "two flower shops, on the east and west coasts of the U.S., connected by telegraph wires. Two globes and a banner" indicated the company's worldwide

a bouquet replaced the box three years later. A golden band encircled the image in 1957, the bouquet became more abundant, and Mercury more refined. Since then the changes to the logo have been minimal; in 1979 "Since 1910" was added to the circle "as an indication of the association's longevity and stability." The company celebrated its 80th birthday in 1998.

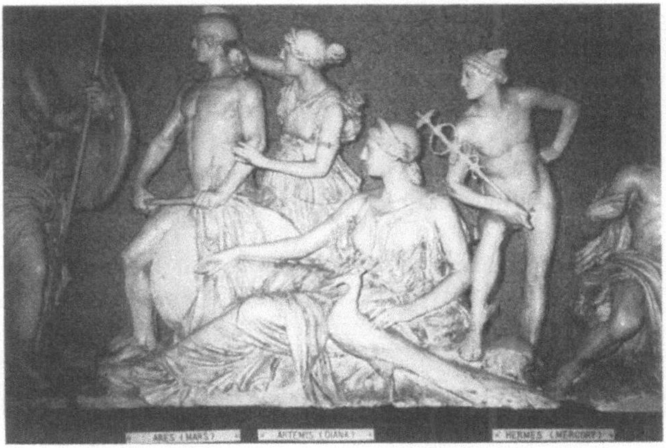

6.3 Hermes: Nashville \ Parthenon

One of the best known brands of haute couture is HERMÈS, French creator of scarves, travel accessories, and perfume. The company introduced a new scent in the early 1990s and gave it a name taken from its logo, *Calèche*, further defining it as *Soie de Parfum*. The name and the logo of the company draws it into this study of mythological echoes.

The HERMÈS logo is more complex than manyothers, for it depicts three fully developed figures: a man, a horse, and an open carriage or calèche. The images are designed to reflect the travel means of the wealthy citizens of Paris in the 18th century and thus indicate that products bearing this logo are indicators of the highest class and taste. It is an exclusive design, one that excludes the ordinary person. As the company's name, that of its founder, is also that of the Greek god who protects travelers of all status and on all of life's journeys — the deity, in the role of

---

flower sending capability. FTD means "Florists' Telegraph Delivery, changed in 1967 to "Florists' Transworld Delivery."

psychopompos, even accompanies a person on the final trip to the realm of the dead—it is appropriate that the HERMÈS logo indicates a journey.

The logo reflects travel in 17th and 18th century Paris: the guide, the horse, and the calèche. HERMÈS was established in 1837 by Thierry Hermès; as he shared the name of Greek god of travel, he maintained it for the company he began for the manufacture and whole selling of harnesses. His son, Emile-Charles, extended the venture to the production of saddles; ensuing generations of the family began making, for those who could afford them, the finest quality leather goods in the world. Soon the company expanded into clothing, much of which bears equestrian symbols. Recently, HERMÈS has added perfumes and ready-to-wear clothing, as well as china and crystal, to its inventory. But the qualities that Thierry Hermès established over 150 years ago still remain the hallmark of the company.[19]

By its clever use of name and myth, HERMÈS of Paris has created a label that can be both exclusive and inclusive. The design of the logo elevates the product, while the name itself suggests that the company's products should be attractive to all people. While, in fact, the high price of a HERMÈS item is prohibitive to all but those with many francs or dollars, the dream is still available. And, after all, Hermes was also the god who guided dreams.

One of the best known logos in the world is that of NIKE. It too, is a winged foot, but over time the foot became ever more stylized, until finally the wordless logo stands as a single wing so recognizable that neither the name of the company nor its products needed to be presented.

The NIKE wing and the company name comes from the Greek goddess Athena Nike, the winged goddess of victory whose small dedicatory temple stands at the far western edge of the Acropolis in Athens. Victory was believed to have wings so she could travel quickly to a battle site and bring aid to the side she favored. The ideas of speed, success, and quick victory appealed to the founders of NIKE who discovered in the ancient symbol a vibrant meaning for their new company.[20]

---

[19] Information on establishment of this company taken from FRANCE Today 10 (September 1995): 8. Hermès did not respond to my inquiries about the origin of its logo.

[20] Information from informational brochure published by NIKE's public relations office and sent to me.

By the late 1990s, however, the wing, now universally called the "swoosh", became too well known, its appearance too wide-spread. The company saw a substantial profit and stock loss in 1997; its stock dropped 50 percent in the first two quarters of 1998. The swoosh, having become almost as ubiquitous as Coca-Cola's name-logo, suddenly was seen where the company did not want it to be: on the new black NIKE's of the suicidal Hale-Bopp comet followers, on the entire wardrobe of a schoolyard killer, on O. J. Simpson's cap. But it was not just the appearance in bad places that hurt NIKE in 1998. The word was out about the company's Asian underpaid workers, its over-expansion into many things not related to sports, its insensitive posters in Paris during the World Cup, even its sponsorship of the Brazilian team in that competition. By the fall of 1998, NIKE's directors were considering a radical step: abandon the swoosh.[21] NIKE had to look back at the wing which gave it victory and reevaluate the responsibilities and liabilities of success. In the end, the swoosh won the victory: it remains the NIKE symbol.

Perugina chocolate boasts a Griffin as its symbol. The fantastic beast is the traditional guardian of the city of Perugia, a symbol which the chocolate company traces back to the city's Etruscan origins. The company's public relations brochure proclaims that the Griffin, a symbolic figure [was] "born in the imagination of antiquity with the features and wings of an eagle and the body of a lion...[which] also guards over Perugia's finest treasure--the delicious confections of Perugina."[22] As the "fabled Griffin loved gold and jewels," so the company loves to put out its candies wrapped in bright papers; Perugina, acting "under the gaze of the Griffin" is devoted to quality. The brochure closes thus: "Look for Perugina's Griffin--always a symbol of taste, quality and beauty."

The Griffin is most commonly associated with eastern kingdoms; it appears on the gates to Babylon, for instance, and on the carvings on the palace at Persepolis. It is interesting that Perugina associates the mythical beast with the Etruscan town of Perugia, for the origin of the Etruscans in Italy is not certainly known, but a migration from the east is the favored explanation for their presence. However, it has also been suggested that the wings of the Perugia Griffin were added in the 1200's to an Etruscan

---

[21] Information on Nike's problems taken from Timothy Egan, "The Swoon of the Swoosh," New York *Times* Magazine (September 13, 1998): 66-70.

[22] The brochure was sent to me by Perugina (without sender's name, 7-18-1995). All information quoted is from that brochure.

bronze lion.[23] Whatever the exact origins of the Griffin, Perugina adopted it for the reasons given above.

A logo is a symbol carefully chosen to represent a company. It must reflect by its image the ideals and values the company wants the public to associatewith its product; indeed, the logo defines the company in both the eye and the mind of the consumer. The classical figures described here were selected for the status they would instantly confer and thus does the power and vitality of Greek and Roman mythology continue to flourish in the modern world.

[23] The Etruscans were masters at bronze working. The symbol of Rome itself, the Capitoline wolf, is an Etruscan creation, as is the fanciful Chimera of Arezzo. Since both real and imaginary animals were created by the Etruscans, either theory could hold true.

VII
CONCLUSION

Advertising, by the general consensus of all who study it, both reflects its times and responds to the desires of its audience. In the late 1930s, for example, companies chose to promote their products in terms of comfortable living and old-fashioned values. As Jackson Lears pointed out, "Advertisers, like other symbol-makers in the 1930s, had turned to a mythic version of the American past to validate their present identity."[1] A social change was necessary, also: families had to want what companies were making. As Andrew Wernick puts it (24):

> . . . Stimulating sufficient demand to absorb the (costly) new cornucopia required not only massive publicity but also radical changes in household habits, spending patterns, and family values. The family had to become a centre of consumption rather than production.[2]

As previously noted, even as early as 1947 it was recognized that a primary function of advertising was to create consumer demands for things people did not know they wanted until advertising invented their desire for them.[3] As we have seen here, the creators of the advertising turned to classical myth to arouse this desire for the new and daring; indeed, in the last years of the 1980s and early years of the 1990s, classical myth permeated print media advertising. It was a time when life was moving very fast, technology was invading every home in ways which had yet to be mastered, when the American belief in "family values" was being challenged even as many sought to restore it.[4] Familiar businesses were merged into large corporations whose identity was almost secret; well-known foods and brands were made by unknown conglomerates. Even in the once rather isolated world of academia, traditional courses were being discarded for new trends and theories:

---

[1]Jackson Lears, *Fables of Abundance: A Cultural History of Advertising in America.* (New York: 1994): 383.

[2] Wernick, *Promotional Culture*: 24.

[3] According to a *Fortune* (November, 1947: 210), magazine study quoted by Thomas Frank, *the conquest of cool.* (Chicago, 1997): 49.

[4] One voice protesting this breakdown of traditional cultural values was that of James Twitchell, who studied this failing of American culture of the last decade in his book *For Shame. The Loss of Common Decency in American Culture*. (New York: St. Martin's, 1997).

students (who came with little historical or cultural background) were being offered classes which discarded past ideas before they had been learned.[5] The world was in flux, but the direction in which things were flowing was uncertain, if not alarming.

Into this unstable world where answers were lacking stepped the advertising agency and its artists. In the ever-more attractive art of the advertisement the American public could find traditional standards of value returned, could find that there are indeed lasting icons of Western culture to provide an anchor in the swift currents that seemed to be carrying away everything familiar. Any person in the street, despite the break-down of traditional education, could recognize the Venus di Milo, or, at least, recognize it as a statue from the ancient world of Greece and Rome. Inside the university the inheritance in the west from Greece and Rome was (far too often) being challenged, but in the "real" world of work and commerce a distant memory of that debt still survived. As James Twitchell has so elegantly reminded us, we live in "Adcult," and in this culture, dominated by advertising, it is in advertising that public values can be affirmed and ascertained.

The creators of the mythological advertisement did make a leap of faith: they assumed that classical learning was not yet dead. While the Venus di Milo is immediately recognizable, at some level, to almost everyone who would be buying the product(s) she endorsed, many of the advertisements, as we have seen, were based on less familiar legends. And the stories themselves were turned; one had to know the original to understand the alteration to get the point of the advertisement. The companies and their agencies knew their targeted audience, of course, and the more sophisticated advertisements were directed to the more sophisticated consumer, or to the consumer who wished to appear more sophisticated. In this latter way, the classical myth served to elevate a buyer's self-status, by acquiring products advertised by mythological reference each shopper could participate in the common cultural values of an educated American public.

As I continued to examine print media advertisements while I completed the research and the manuscript for this book, it became evident that in the last years of the 1990s, in the closing years of the century, ancient myth seemed to play a lesser role. The careful reader will have noticed that the majority of my examples come from the years 1990-1996; that reader may have assumed that I laid aside the glossy magazines and turned away my eager mythology students. Neither is true. Thus I

[5] For a searing indictment of the failure of academia to offer solid (western) cultural values, see Victor Hanson and John Heath, *Who Killed Homer?* (New York et al: The Free Press, 1998) passim.

was compelled to ponder why Madison Avenue looked less often to the Greek and Roman world for inspiration.[6]

In the first place, it seemed that the more recent magazine advertisements reflected the stories created by the commercials appearing on television, where in ever-shorter moments mini-dramas were played out.[7] These quick scenes of interaction could seldom retell the old stories, but had to portray scenes of immediately recognized everyday life, and very frequently relied on humor to make the mini-scenes memorable. While the turn of a Greek myth can be funny, the minute or less run time of the television commercial did not permit any such extended development. But there are other reasons, I think to the decline of ancient myth in the most contemporary American advertising; my quest must look beyond the influence of television. For not only are the products advertised in the print media in many instances not those shown on the television screen, the static image makes a different impact and offers its message in a special way.

A rather disheartening response might lie in the widespread and often strident demands of multiculturalism, a point of view that in many instances denies the influence of the classical world on western culture. In seeking to promote the value of cultures other than European, especially African heritage, the voices of multicultural studies have attracted attention both within the academy and without.

---

[6] Although Greek myth appeared less often in print media advertisements, it did not fade from American culture. Each and every afternoon children's television featured (ever new and not really Greek) adventures of Hercules, while the play earning rave reviews on Broadway in 1998-1999 was David Leveaux's production of Sophocles' *Electra*, starring Zoe Wannamaker in the title role. And it was only four years earlier that Euripides' *Medea*, starring Diana Rigg, won the Tony Award for best play on Broadway in 1994.

[7] One of the first (if not the first) use of the mini-drama was that designed by the Cabot Advertising Agency of Boston for New England Telephone. In 1988 the campaign, broadcast over a six month period, told a story wherein a telephone call healed a breach between father and daughter. Joanne Morreale and Karen Buzzard argue that such stories serve "only to perpetuate cultural illusions...imply that using a commodity can make one's life better," and conclude that in the mini-drama "advertisers appropriate the moral injunctions of allegory in order to make needs and desires into objects of consumption." Morreale and Buzzard, "The Serialized Mini-Drama: A New Trend in Advertising," in Danna, Sammy, Ed. *Advertising and Popular Culture. Studies in Variety and Versatility*. Bowling Green, OH: Bowling Green State University Press (1992): 101-102. I cite their comments here because they include allegory among the techniques used by advertisers to influence the buyer, and allegory and myth are closely related.

When Martin Bernal's *Black Athena* becomes the subject of newspaper articles and television specials, as well as conference sessions (and books attacking his thesis), it might seem dangerous to promote women's lingerie beside the Parthenon, a building which may seem to some to be a symbol of white male aggression.

But I prefer a more positive response. Many print media advertisements in the late 1990s certainly rely no less upon a sexual allure, but now an allure no longer masked by classical allusion. Others, however, look to a realm of myth other than the ancient Greek. They look to American myth, the myth of the family as a happy unit, families of all races as happy consumers of the good life as Americans have defined it. As the century draws to a close, when it seems that society's traditional ideas have slipped away, when more than fifty percent of marriages end in divorce and more than one in three children live in a home with only one biological parent, a wave of nostalgia has once again swept over America. Fashions of the fifties are back, in dress, in food, in cars--witness the return of the Volkswagen beetle (albeit a larger bug engineered differently)--, even homes are being laid out in retrograde design. And none of this is unusual or unexpected. The veil of time hides what people in the 1960s rebelled against and in the 70s and 80s remembered unhappily about the 1950s; the recalled images show a time when security and trust were more common, when the family was a secure unit.

Advertising has always shown us a world where we would like to be, it creates desires for a life style to which we would aspire.[8] In the early years of the 1990s decade, that world was one defined by glamour, by art, by high culture, by an exclusivity attained by education, or at least a veneer of culture based on a western world view of what had lasting value. The years, too, were marked by changing times, and the classics from Greece and Rome offered an anchor and a guide against which new arrivals into the upper classes could measure their success. A home with Grecian columns, perfumes and make-up which gave their wearer instant class, the use of a product advertised as atop a column: these assured the American consumers that they had arrived. Some twenty years ago Varda Langholz- Leymore asserted the similarity between the roles of myth and advertising in modern America, as myths serve to support social order and resolve social contradictions, so does advertising. The latter, she asserted, solves life's four great problems: "one will belong rather than be excluded, one will have happiness rather than misery,

[8] For a rather elegant exposition of the role of advertising and the American Dream (*sic*), see the closing pages of Juliann Sivulka, *Soap, Sex and Cigarettes* (Belmont, CA et al: Wadsworth, 1998): 425-428. Sivulka's entire text is well worth reading.

good rather than evil, life rather than death."[9] As the Muse walked Madison Avenue she gave direction to the designers of American advertising, and by underlining the American myth, through their work she gave definition to the American dream.

In the closing years of the decade, the Muse still assists those who create the advertisements which encourage and induce us to be consumers, to buy products which will enhance our lives. When Hesiod recorded that the Muses appeared to him on the slopes of Mt. Helicon to guide his writing of the *Theogony,* the story of the world's generation and the gods which direct it, it was the myths of his society which he recorded. Today the Muses teach the myths of our times to writers in all genre: poetry, novels, plays, and, in a special way, advertising. For as early societies and especially the ancient Greeks understood, it is a community's myths that sustain a common social order.

The influence of Greece and Rome via the legends and architecture that were created during the classical period is and will always be a part of western culture. At times this influence has stood front and center, at other timesit has stepped back into the shadows, allowing other newer ideas to hold the stage. But in future decades the classical ideal will be recalled to add its glamour to American products and designs, for ancient Greece and Rome have played a major role in theculture of the American marketplace. Then once more the classical Muse will return to Madison Avenue.

---

[9] Varda Langholz-Leymore, *Hidden Myth: Structure and Symbolism in Advertising.* (London Heinemann Educational Books, 1975): 156. Ronald Berman, *Advertising and Social Change* (Beverly Hills: 1981): 47, also citing (Langholz-)Leymore, adds that advertising "sells the mundane but invokes the fabulous." That also describes the role of myth: to dictate proper and ordinary behavior with stories that excite wonder. William M. O'Barr, *Culture and the Ad. Exploring Otherness in the World of Advertising* (Boulder et al: Westview Press, 1994), closes his study by asserting that "this discourse [of advertising] reflects social practices and cultural values already present, [and it also] recreates them in the process of depicting them" (206).

ILLUSTRATIONS

ILLUSTRATIONS: CHAPTER II

ILLUSTRATIONS: CHAPTER III

ILLUSTRATIONS: CHAPTER IV

ILLUSTRATIONS: CHAPTER V

ILLUSTRATIONS: CHAPTER VI

Total: **76**

MUSE ON MADISON AVENUE

BIBLIOGRAPHY

Berman, Ronald. *Advertising and Social Change*. Beverly Hills, CA: Sage Publications (1981).

Damon-Moore, Helen. *Magazines for the Millions. Gender and Commerce in the Ladies' Home Journal and the Saturday Evening Post, 1889-1910.* Albany, NY: SUNY (1994).

Danna, Sammy, Ed. *Advertising and Popular Culture. Studies in Variety and Versatility.* Bowling Green, OH: Bowling Green State University Press (1992).

DeLong, Marilyn Revell and Elizabeth Kersch Bye. Apparel for the Senses: The Use and Meaning of Fragrances," *Journal of Popular Culture* 24 (3/Winter, 1990): 81-88.

Dotz, Warren, and Jim Morton. *What a Character! 20th Century American Advertising Icons.* San Francisco, CA: Chronicle Books (1996)

Ewen, Stuart and Elizabeth. *Channels of Desire. Mass Media and the Shaping of the American Consciousness* New York: McGraw-Hill (1982).

Fox, Stephen. *The Mirror Makers. A History of American Advertising and its Creators.* New York: Morrow (1984).

Frank, Thomas. *The Conquest of Cool. Business culture, Counterculture, and the Rise of Hip Consumerism.* Chicago, IL: University of Chicago Press (1997).

Goffman, Erving. *Gender Advertisements*. Cambridge, MA: Harvard (1979).

Gold, Philip. *Advertising, Politics, and American Culture.* From *Salesmanship to Therapy.* New York: Paragon House (1987).

Hall, Dennis, "Advertising as High Art," *The Mid-Atlantic Almanack* 4 (1995): 54-60.

Hine, Thomas, "Notable Quotables: Why Images Become Icons," *New York Times* (February 18, 1996): 1/37.

Hine, Thomas. *The Total Package. The Secret History and Hidden Meanings of Boxes, Bottles, Cans, and Other Persuasive Containers.* Boston et al: Little Brown & Company (1995).

Hovland, R. & Gary Wilcox, ed. *Advertising in Society. Classic and Contemporary Readings on Advertising's Role in Society.* Lincolnwood, IL: NTC Business Books (1990).

Hubbard, Rita C. "Shock Advertising: The BENETTON Case," *SPC* 16 (1993): 39-51.

Langholz-Leymore, Varda. *Hidden Myth: Structure and Symbolism in Advertising.* London: Heinemann Educational Books (1975).

Laurenceau, Thomas. *RÉMY MARTIN. L'ESPRIT DU COGNAC* (Paris: E.P.A., 1991): 19-22.

Lears, T.J. Jackson. *Fables of Abundance: A Cultural History of Advertising in America.* New York: Basic Books (1994).

Levitt, Theodore, "The Morality (?) of Advertising," *Harvard Business Review (July-August, 1972), rep. Advertising's Role in Society.* Ed. John S. Wright and John E. Mertes. St. Paul, MN: West Publishing (1974): 278-289.

Manca, Luigi. "Images of Yuppies in Popular Advertisements of the 1980s," in Sammy Danna, Ed. *Advertising and Popular Culture. Studies in Variety and Versatility.* Bowling Green, OH: Bowling Green State University Press (1992): 47-55.

Millum, Trevor. *Images of Woman. Advertising in Women's Magazines.* Totowa, NJ: Rowman and Littlefield (1975).

Norris, James D. *Advertising and the Transformation of American Society, 1865-1920.* Westport, CT: Greenwood (1990).

O'Barr. William M. *Culture and the Ad. Exploring Otherness in the World of Advertising.* Boulder, CO: Westview Press (1994).

Olson, Alan, M. ed. *Myth, Symbol and Reality.* Notre Dame, IN: University Press (1980).

Pollay, Richard. "Quality of Life in the Padded Sell: Common Criticisms of Advertising's Cultural Character and International Public Policies," in *Current Issues & Research in Advertising* 9 (1986): 173-250.

Pollay, Richard. "The Distorted Mirror: Reflections on the Unintended Consequences of Advertising," in *Advertising in Society. Classic and Contemporary Readings on Advertising's Role in Society.* Edited by Roxanne Hovland and Gary B. Wilcox. Lincolnwood, IL: NTC Business Books (1990): 437-476.

Randazzo, Sal. *Mythmaking on Madison Avenue. How Advertisers Apply the Power of Myth and Symbolism to Create Leadership Brands.* Chicago, IL: Probus (1993).

Room, Adrian. *Dictionary of Trade Name Origins.* London: Routledge & Kegan Paul (1982).

Sinclair, John. *Images Incorporated: Advertising as Industry and Ideology.* London & New York: Croom Helm (1987).

Sivulka, Juliann. *Soap, Sex, and Cigarettes. A Cultural History of American Advertising.* Belmont, CA et al: Wadsworth Publishing Co. (1998).

Strasser, Susan. *Satisfaction Guaranteed: The Making of the American Mass Market.* New York: Pantheon (1989).

Twitchell, James. *Adcult USA. The Triumph of Advertising in American Culture.* New York: Columbia University Press (1996).

Twitchell, James. *For Shame. The Loss of Common Decency in American Culture.* New York: St. Martin's, (1997).

Wernick, Andrew. *Promotional Culture. Advertising, ideology and symbolic expression.* London: Sage Publications (1991).

Whipple, Thomas. "The Existence and Effectiveness of Sexual Content in Advertising," in *Advertising and Popular Culture. Studies in Variety and Versatility.* Ed. Sammy Dana. Bowling Green, OH: Bowling Green State University (1992): 134-140.

Wicke, Jennifer. *Advertising Fictions. Literature, Advertisement, & Social Reading.* New York: Columbua University Press, (1988).

Wright, John S. and John E. Mertes, Ed. *Advertising's Role in Society.* St. Paul, MN: West Publishing (1974).

Zelman, Tom, "Language and Perfume" in *Advertising and Popular Culture. Studies in Variety and Versatility.* Ed. Sammy Dana. Bowling Green, OH: Bowling Green State University (1992): 109-114.

INDEX

C

N

O

P

R

S

T

STUDIEN ZUR KLASSISCHEN PHILOLOGIE

Herausgegeben von Michael von Albrecht

Band 1 Ulrike Kettemann: Interpretationen zu Satz und Vers in Ovids erotischem Lehrgedicht. 1979.

Band 2 Walter Kißel: Das Geschichtsbild des Silius Italicus. 1979.

Band 3 Peter Smith: Nursling of Mortality. A Study of the Homeric Hymn to Aphrodite. 1981.

Band 4 Änne Bäumer: Die Bestie Mensch. Senecas Aggressionstheorie, ihre philosophischen Vorstufen und ihre literarischen Auswirkungen. 1982.

Band 5 Christiane Reitz: Die Nekyia in den Punica des Silius Italicus. 1982.

Band 6 Markus Weber: Die mythologische Erzählung in Ovids Liebeskunst. Verankerung, Struktur und Funktion. 1983.

Band 7 Karin Neumeister: Die Überwindung der elegischen Liebe bei Properz. (Buch I - III). 1983.

Band 8 Werner Schubert: Jupiter in den Epen der Flavierzeit. 1984.

Band 9 Dorothea Koch-Peters: Ansichten des Orosius zur Geschichte seiner Zeit. 1984.

Band 10 Bernd Heßen: Der historische Infinitiv im Wandel der Darstellungstechnik Sallusts. 1984.

Band 11 Cornelia Renger: Aeneas und Turnus. Analyse einer Feindschaft. 1985.

Band 12 Reinhold Glei: Die Batrachomyomachie. Synoptische Edition und Kommentar. 1984.

Band 13 Nikolaos Tachinoslis: Handschriften und Ausgaben der Odyssee. Mit einem Handschriftenapparat zu Allen´s Odysseeausgabe. 1984.

Band 14 S. Georgia Nugent: Allegory and Poetics. The Structure and Imagery of Prudentius´ *Psychomachia*. 1985.

Band 15 Anton D. Leeman: Form und Sinn. Studien zur römischen Literatur (1954-1984). 1985.

Band 16 Wolfgang Hübner: Die Petronübersetzung Wilhelm Heinses. Quellenkritisch bearbeiteter Nachdruck der Erstausgabe mit textkritisch-exegetischem Kommentar. (Band I-II). 1986.

Band 17 Roland Glaesser: Verbrechen und Verblendung. Untersuchung zum Furor-Begriff bei Lucan mit Berücksichtigung der Tragödien Senecas. 1984.

Band 18 Fritz-Heiner Mutschler: Die poetische Kunst Tibulls. Struktur und Bedeutung der Bücher 1 und 2 des Corpus Tibullianum. 1985.

Band 19 Rismag Gordesiani: Kriterien der Schriftlichkeit und Mündlichkeit im homerischen Epos. 1986.

Band 20 Madeleine Mary Henry: Menander´s Courtesans and the Greek Comic Tradition. 1985. 2. Auflage 1988.

Band 21 Bernd Janson: Etymologische und chronologische Untersuchungen zu den Bedingungen des Rhotazismus im Albanischen unter Berücksichtigung der griechischen und lateinischen Lehnwörter. 1986.

Band 22 Ernst A. Schmidt: Bukolische Leidenschaft - oder Über antike Hirtenpoesie. 1987.

Band 23 Pedro C. Tapia Zúñiga: Vorschlag eines Lexikons zu den Aitia des Kallimachos. Buchstabe "Alpha". 1986.

Band 24 Eberhard Heck: MH ΘΕΟΜΑΧΕΙΝ oder: Die Bestrafung des Gottesverächters. Untersuchungen zu Bekämpfung und Aneignung römischer religio bei Tertullian, Cyprian und Lactanz. 1987.

Band 25 Manfred Gerhard Schmidt: Caesar und Cleopatra. Philologischer und historischer Kommentar zu Lucan. 10,1-171. 1986.

Band 26 Wolfgang Jäger: Briefanalysen. Zum Zusammenhang von Realitätserfahrung und Sprache in Briefen Ciceros. 1986.

Band 27 Lewis A. Sussman: The Major Declamations Ascribed to Quintilian. A Translation. 1987.

Band 28 Klaus Kubusch: Aurea Saecula: Mythos und Geschichte. Untersuchung eines Motivs in der antiken Literatur bis Ovid. 1986.

Band 29 Helmut Mauch: O laborum dulce lenimen. Funktionsgeschichtliche Untersuchungen zur römischen Dichtung zwischen Republik und Prinzipat am Beispiel der ersten Odensammlung des Horaz. 1986.

Band 30 Karl Meister: Studien zu Sprache, Literatur und Religion der Römer. Herausgegeben von Viktor Pöschl und Michael von Albrecht. 1987.

Band 31 Hubert Müller: Früher Humanismus in Oberitalien. Albertino Mussato: Ecerinis. 1987.

Band 32 Andrea Scheithauer: Kaiserbild und literarisches Programm. Untersuchungen zur Tendenz der Historia Augusta. 1987.

Band 33 Carlos J. Larrain: Die Sentenzen des Porphyrios. Handschriftliche Überlieferung. Die Übersetzung von Marsilio Ficino. Deutsche Übersetzung. 1987.

Band 34 Catherine J. Castner: Prosopography of Roman Epicureans from the Second Century B.C. to the Second Century A.D. 2nd unchanged edition. 1991.

Band 35 Gabriele Möhler: Hexameterstudien zu Lukrez, Vergil, Horaz, Ovid, Lukan, Silius Italicus und der Ilias Latina. 1989.

Band 36 Clara-Emmanuelle Auvray: Folie et Douleur dans Hercule Furieux et Hercule sur l'Oeta. Recherches sur l'expression esthétique de l'ascèse stoïcienne chez Sénèque. 1989.

Band 37 Thomas Weber: Fidus Achates. Der Gefährte des Aeneas in Vergils Aeneis. 1988.

Band 38 Waltraut Desch: Augustins Confessiones. Beobachtungen zu Motivbestand und Gedankenbewegung. 1988.

Band 39 Maria-Barbara Quint: Untersuchungen zur mittelalterlichen Horaz-Rezeption. 1988.

Band 40 Eugene Michael O'Connor: Symbolum Salacitatis. A Study of the God Priapus as a Literary Character. 1989.

Band 41 Michael von Albrecht: Scripta Latina. Accedunt variorum Carmina Heidelbergensia dissertatiunculae colloquia. 1989.

Band 42 Werner Rutz: Studien zur Kompositionskunst und zur epischen Technik Lucans. Herausgegeben und mit einem bibliographischen Nachwort versehen von Andreas W. Schmitt. 1989.

Band 43 Henri Le Bonniec: Etudes ovidiennes. Introduction aux *Fastes* d'Ovide. 1989.

Band 44 Stefan Merkle: Die Ephemeris belli Troiani des Diktys von Kreta. 1989.

Band 45 Michael Gagarin: The Murder of Herodes. A Study of Antiphon 5. 1989.

Band 46 Joachim Fugmann: Königszeit und Frühe Republik in der Schrift *De viris illustribus urbis Romae.* Quellenkritisch-historische Untersuchungen. 1990.

Band 47 Sabine Grebe: Die vergilische Heldenschau. Tradition und Fortwirken. 1989.

Band 48 Bardo Maria Gauly: Liebeserfahrungen. Zur Rolle des elegischen Ich in Ovids Amores. 1990.

Band 49 Jörg Maurer: Untersuchungen zur poetischen Technik und den Vorbildern der Ariadne-Epistel Ovids.1990.

Band 50 Karelisa V. Hartigan: Ambiguity and Self-Deception. The Apollo and Artemis Plays of Euripides. 1991.

Band 51 Hermann Lind: Der Gerber Kleon in den 'Rittern' des Aristophanes. Studien zur Demagogenkomödie. 1990.

Band 52 Alexandra Bartenbach: Motiv- und Erzählstruktur in Ovids Metamorphosen. Das Verhältnis von Rahmen- und Binnenerzählungen im 5., 10. und 15. Buch von Ovids Metamorphosen. 1990.

Band 53 Jürgen Schmidt: Lukrez, der Kepos und die Stoiker. Untersuchungen zur Schule Epikurs und zu den Quellen von *De rerum natura.* 1990.

Band 54 Martin Glatt: Die 'andere Welt' der römischen Elegiker. Das Persönliche in der Liebesdichtung. 1991.

Band 55 John F. Miller: Ovid's Elegiac Festivals. Studies in the *Fasti.* 1991.

Band 56 Elisabeth Vandiver: Heroes in Herodotus. The Interaction of Myth and History. 1991.

Band 57 Frank-Joachim Simon: Τὰ κύλλ ' ἀείδειν. Interpretationen zu den Mimiamben des Herodas. 1991.

Band 58 Arthur J. Pomeroy: The Appropriate Comment. Death Notices in the Ancient historians. 1991.

Band 59 Martina Kötzle: Weibliche Gottheiten in Ovids Fasten. 1991.

Band 60 Glynn Meter: Walter of Châtillon's Alexandreis Book 10–A commentary. 1991.

Band 61 Burghard Schröder: Carmina non quae nemorale resultent. Ein Kommentar zur 4. Ekloge des Calpurnius Siculus. 1991.

Band 62 Michele V. Ronnick: Cicero's Paradoxa Stoicorum. A Commentary, an Interpretation and a Study of Its Influence. 1991.

Band 63 Mary Frances Williams: Landscape in the *Argonautica* of Apollonius Rhodius. 1992.

Band 64 Christine Walde: Herculeus labor. Studien zum pseudosenecanischen Hercules Oetaeus. 1992.

Band 65 Anna Elissa Radke: Harmonica vitrea. 1992.

Band 66 Werner Schubert: Die Mythologie in den nichtmythologischen Dichtungen Ovids. 1992.

Band 67 Karl Galinsky (Hrsg.): The interpretation of Roman poetry. Empiricism or hermeneutics? 1992.

Band 68 Alexander Kessissoglu: Die fünfte Vorrede in Vitruvs De architectura. 1993.

Band 69 Peter Prestel: Die Rezeption der ciceronischen Rhetorik durch Augustinus in De doctrina Christiana. 1992.

Band 70 Ursula Hecht: Der Pluto furens des Petrus Martyr Anglerius. Dichtung als Dokumentation. 1992.

Band 71 Richard Laqueur: Diodors Geschichtswerk. Die Überlieferung von Buch I - V. Aus dem Nachlaß herausgegeben von Kai Brodersen. 1992.

Band 72 Christine Korten: Ovid, Augustus und der Kult der Vestalinnen. Eine religionspolitische These zur Verbannung Ovids. 1992.

Band 73 Kurt Scheidle: Modus optumum. Die Bedeutung des "rechten Maßes" in der römischen Literatur (Republik – frühe Kaiserzeit), untersucht an den Begriffen Modus – Modestia – Moderatio – Temperantia. 1993.

Band 74 Sibylle Tochtermann: Der allegorisch gedeutete Kirke-Mythos. Studien zur Entwicklungs- und Rezeptionsgeschichte. 1992.

Band 75 Hansgerd Frank: *Ratio* bei Cicero. 1992.

Band 76 Günter Klause: Die Periphrase der Nomina propria bei Vergil. 1993.

Band 77 Jelle Bouma: Marcus Iunius Nypsus – Fluminis Varatio / Limitis Repositio. Introduction, Text, Translation and Commentary. 1993.

Band 78 Sabine Rochlitz: Das Bild Caesars in Ciceros *Orationes Caesarianae.* Untersuchungen zur *clementia* und *sapientia Caesaris.* 1993.

Band 79 Anna Lydia Motto / John R. Clark: Essays on Seneca. 1993.

Band 80 Ernst Zinn: Viva Vox. Römische Klassik und deutsche Dichtung. 1993.

Band 81 Hee-Seong Kim: Die Geisttaufe des Messias. Eine kompositionsgeschichtliche Untersuchung zu einem Leitmotiv des lukanischen Doppelwerks. Ein Beitrag zur Theologie und Intention des Lukas. 1993.

Band 82 Tilmann Leidig: Valerius Antias und ein annalistischer Bearbeiter des Polybios als Quellen des Livius, vornehmlich für Buch 30 und 31. 1994.

Band 83 Thomas Zinsmaier: Der von Bord geworfene Leichnam. Die sechste der neunzehn größeren pseudoquintilianischen Deklamationen. Einleitung, Übersetzung, Kommentar. 1993.

Band 84 Victoria Tietze Larson: The Role of Description in Senecan Tragedy. 1994.

Band 85 Eugen Braun: Lukian. Unter doppelter Anklage. Ein Kommentar. 1994.

Band 86 Sabine Wedner: Tradition und Wandel im allegorischen Verständnis des Sirenenmythos. Ein Beitrag zur Rezeptionsgeschichte Homers. 1994.

Band 87 Karlhermann Bergner: Der Sapientia-Begriff im Kommentar des Marius Victorinus zu Ciceros Jugendwerk *De Inventione.* 1994.

Band 88 Angelika Seibel: Volksverführung als schöne Kunst. Die Diapeira im zweiten Gesang der Ilias als ein Lehrstück demagogischer Ästhetik. 1994.

Band 89 Gabriele Ledworuski: Historiographische Widersprüche in der Monographie Sallusts zur Catilinarischen Verschwörung. 1994.

Band 90 Aldo Setaioli: La vicenda dell'anima nel commento di Servio a Virgilio. 1995.

Band 91 James S. Hirstein: Tacitus' Germania and Beatus Rhenanus (1485-1547). A Study of the Editorial and Exegetical Contribution of a Sixteenth Century Scholar. 1995.

Band 92 Thomas Stäcker: Die Stellung der Theurgie in der Lehre Jamblichs. 1995.

Band 93 Egert Pöhlmann: Studien zur Bühnendichtung und zum Theaterbau der Antike. 1995.

Band 94 Barbara Feichtinger: Apostolae apostolorum. Frauenaskese als Befreiung und Zwang bei Hieronymus. 1995.

Band 95 Andreas W. Schmitt: Die direkten Reden der Massen in Lucans Pharsalia. 1995.

Band 96 Burkard Chwalek: Die Verwandlung des Exils in die elegische Welt. Studien zu den *Tristia* und *Epistulae ex Ponto* Ovids. 1996.

Band 97 Axel Sütterlin: Petronius Arbiter und Federico Fellini. Ein strukturanalytischer Vergleich. 1996.

Band 98 Oleg Nikitinski: Kallimachos-Studien. 1996.

Band 99 Christiane Reitz: Zur Gleichnistechnik des Apollonios von Rhodos. 1996.

Band 100 Werner Schubert (Hrsg.): Ovid – Werk und Wirkung. Festgabe für Michael von Albrecht zum 65. Geburtstag. 1999.

Band 101 Martin Korenjak: Die Ericthoszene in Lukans *Pharsalia.* Einleitung, Text, Übersetzung, Kommentar. 1996.

Band 102 Sabine Schäfer: Das Weltbild der Vergilischen *Georgika* in seinem Verhältnis zu *De rerum natura* des Lukrez. 1996.

Band 103 Andreas Pronay (Hrsg.): C. Marius Victorinus: Liber de definitionibus. Eine spätantike Theorie der Definition und des Definierens. Mit Einleitung, Übersetzung und Kommentar. 1997.

Band 104 Paola Migliorini: Scienza e terminologia medica nella letteratura di età neroniana. Seneca, Lucano, Persio, Petronio. 1997.

Band 105 Eva-Carin Gerö: Negatives and Noun Phrases in Classical Greek. An Investigation Based on the *Corpus Platonicum*. 1997.

Band 106 Mercedes Mauch: Senecas Frauenbild in den philosophischen Schriften. 1997.

Band 107 Threni magistri nostri Ioannis Eckii in obitu Margaretae concubinae suae. Untersucht, ediert, übersetzt und kommentiert von Franz Wachinger. 1997.

Band 108 Roland Granobs: Studien zur Darstellung römischer Geschichte in Ovids *Metamorphosen*. 1997.

Band 109 Diane Bitzel: Bernardo Zamagna "Navis Aëria". Eine Metamorphose des Lehrgedichts im Zeichen des technischen Fortschritts. 1997.

Band 110 Joachim Fugmann: Königszeit und Frühe Republik in der Schrift *De viris illustribus urbis Romae*. Quellenkritisch-historische Untersuchung. II,1: Frühe Republik (6./5. Jh.). 1997.

Band 111 Paul Größlein: Untersuchungen zum *Juppiter confutatus* Lukians. 1998.

Band 112 Jula Wildberger: Ovids Schule der 'elegischen' Liebe. Erotodidaxe und Psychagogie in der *Ars amatoria*. 1998.

Band 113 Andreas Haltenhoff: Kritik der akademischen Skepsis. Ein Kommentar zu Cicero, Lucullus 1-62. 1998.

Band 114 Wolfgang Fauth: Carmen magicum. Das Thema der Magie in der Dichtung der römischen Kaiserzeit. 1999.

Band 115 Rosario Guarino Ortega: Los comentarios al *Ibis* de Ovidio. El largo recorrido de una exégesis. 1999.

Band 116 Francesca Prescendi: Frühzeit und Gegenwart. Eine Studie zur Auffassung und Gestaltung der Vergangenheit in Ovids *Fastorum libri*. 2000.

Band 117 Hans Bernsdorff: Kunstwerke und Verwandlungen. Vier Studien zu ihrer Darstellung im Werk Ovids. 2000.

Band 118 Milena Minkova: The Personal Names of the Latin Inscriptions in Bulgaria. 2000.

Band 119 Aurora López / Andrés Pociña: Estudios sobre comedia romana. 2000.

Band 120 Martina Erdmann: Überredende Reden in Vergils Aeneis. 2000.

Band 121 Frank Beutel: Vergangenheit als Politik. Neue Aspekte im Werk des jüngeren Plinius. 2000.

Band 122 Anna Lydia Motto: Further Essays on Seneca. 2000.

Band 123 Javier Velaza: *Itur in antiquam silvam*. Un estudio sobre la tradición antigua del texto de Virgilio. 2001.

Band 124 William E. Wycislo: Seneca's Epistolary *Responsum*. The *De Ira* as Parody. 2001.

Band 125 Christopher Nappa: Aspects of Catullus' Social Fiction. 2001.

Band 126 Christopher Francese: Parthenius of Nicaea and Roman Poetry. 2001.

Band 127 Karelisa V. Hartigan: Muse on Madison Avenue. Classical Mythology in Contemporary Advertising. 2002.

Band 128 Milena Minkova: The Protean *Ratio.* Notio verbi *rationis* ab Ioanne Scotto Eriugena ad Thomam Aquinatem (synchronice et diachronice). 2001.

Band 129 Antje Schäfer: Vergils Eklogen 3 und 7 in der Tradition der lateinischen Streitdichtung. Eine Darstellung anhand ausgewählter Texte der Antike und des Mittelalters. 2001.

Band 130 Christian Rudolf Raschle: Pestes Harenae. Die Schlangenepisode in Lucans Pharsalia (IX 587-949). Einleitung, Text, Übersetzung, Kommentar. 2001.

Band 131 Jörg Schulte-Altedorneburg: Geschichtliches Handeln und tragisches Scheitern. Herodots Konzept historiographischer Mimesis. 2001.

Band 132 Sivlia Strodel: Zur Überlieferung und zum Verständnis der hellenistischen Technopaignien. 2002.

Band 133 Francis Robert Schwartz: Lucans Tempusgebrauch. Textsyntax und Erzählkunst. 2002.

Bestellungen: Verlag Peter Lang AG, Jupiterstr. 15, CH-3015 Bern, Switzerland